BATH
DESIGN

CONCEPTS, IDEAS, AND PROJECTS

PHILIP MAZZURCO

WHITNEY LIBRARY OF DESIGN
An imprint of Watson-Guptill Publications
New York

A QUARTO BOOK

Copyright © 1986 by Quarto Marketing Ltd.

Library of Congress Catalog Number
85-52136

ISBN: 0-8230-7069-7

BATH DESIGN: Concepts, Ideas, and Projects
was prepared and produced by
Quarto Marketing Ltd.
15 West 26th Street
New York, N.Y. 10010

Editor: Mary Forsell
Designer: Rod Gonzalez
Photo Researcher: Susan M. Duane

Typeset by BPE Graphics, Inc.
Color separations by Hong Kong Scanner Craft Co.
Printed and bound in Hong Kong by Leefung-Asco Printers Ltd.

Cover photograph by Jaime Ardiles-Arce

For Robert

For those whose special efforts above and beyond the call of duty contributed to the success of this project, including Maurice Plourde, Luci Globus, Lisa Walborsky, Ira Stein, and Dinah Paul. For the picture research efforts of Claire Shelley, Bridget Leicester, Katherine Paige—and especially Roger Gross, Jaime Ardiles-Arce, and Timothy Hursley. And for my editors Marta Hallett and Mary Forsell, who managed both steadfastness and humor with deference to both the author and his prevailing deadlines.

CONTENTS

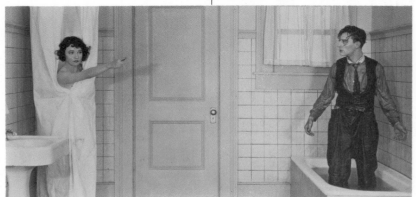

INTRODUCTION

Domestic architecture reveals many confidential things about the social life of the past and present. It amplifies and illuminates the story of civilization and provides an intimate, personal record of habits, postures, manners, fashions, and follies. Materials used for furniture, the methods and processes of decoration, and the origins and character of ornament all give a vivid account of everything from the battle for warmth and privacy to the struggle for dignity and comfort and even of the slower improvement in personal cleanliness.

Although cleanliness is innate in most animals, it is not so in man; notions of cleanliness have to be implanted. A perhaps less-than-respectable generalization, it should nonetheless be noted that the act of bathing enjoyed its own ups and downs—some glorious times of true bathing alternating with long stretches of nonbathing. It should come as no surprise, that although we now consider bathing to be one of the cornerstones of decent living, throughout history, it was more frequently the prerogative of rank rather than common necessity.

Water for personal use often played a neglected tertiary role behind economic survival and tactical warfare. For ancient nomadic tribes, water was so scarce that the defense of a clean watering place was something of a sacred duty; between feuding hordes, cutting off the enemy's water supply would always ensure a strategic victory. When the benefits of personal cleanliness finally were recognized, the people of these tribes often bathed in asses' milk or alkaline mixtures such as soda ash.

2000 B.C.–1501 B.C. While the ancient Egyptians enjoyed the agricultural benefits of the Nile, they also bathed in it. Despite their advanced knowledge of hydraulics, however, the conveyance of water through channels was confined largely to irrigation. This was an arduous task and, even with slaves, was improbable over long distances. The Egyptians, therefore, had to rely on perfumes and ointments to beautify their bodies.

Later and quite separately, a remarkable civilization flourished in the Indus Valley, in what is now Pakistan. Great dome-shaped bathhouses proclaim the memory of a wealthy, disciplined, and domesticated society where public bathing in heated water was almost certainly part of a religious ceremony rather than a reflection of the desire to be clean.

Evidence of man's earliest achievements in hydraulics and sanitary engineering also can be seen on the island of Crete in the Mediterranean. For his palace at Knossos, King Minos installed an ingenious system of sinks, water closets, and cisterns linked with pipes made of terra-cotta. The beauty of these royals baths and the intricacy of Minoan plumbing was unrivaled for hundreds of years thereafter.

But the regularity of bathing suggested by evidence from the Indus Valley and Crete was certainly foreign to the Greeks of Athens. An essentially militaristic society, the Athenians scorned private domestic luxury; baths were taken after competitive athletics and were invariably cold. Not to be underestimated, it was the feat of heating water that would open a new chapter in man's life as we shall see with the Romans.

315 B.C.–A.D. 476. It was, nonetheless, several hundred years before the Romans discarded the asceticism they had inherited from the Greeks. Since Rome was a mercantile and military power rather than an industrial one, peace and prosperity encouraged citizens to develop an agreeable way of life. Domestic comforts and aesthetic pleasures became full-time pursuits. Fusing this new social awareness with their considerable technical ingenuity, the Romans saw a trip to the public baths as a *de rigueur* afternoon activity enlivened by social as well as carnal pleasures. The baths were more than just a social catalyst, they also reflected a new mentality. The Romans also endorsed a program of public-convenience facilities with gusto—Rome had 144 public latrines as early as 315 B.C. Even overseas army barracks, such as Hadrian's Wall across northern England, had multiholers flushed with used water from the bathhouses.

A complex network of aqueducts conveyed the water over long distances and difficult terrain. The bathhouses were as much a new social custom as a vehicle for imperial excess; Emperors Caracalla and Diocletian commissioned huge edifices to accommodate thousands of bathers. While some of these buildings were heated by hot springs such as those at Bath in England, others, such as the Baths of Hadrian in Rome, employed huge fires beneath the terra-cotta tiles of the pools. Besides offering plenty of opportunity for relaxation, the Roman baths also housed shops, libraries, and even museums. Bathing now epitomized the ideal of Roman life—a healthy mind in a healthy body.

The self-assurance of Roman society was largely responsible for its advanced quality of life. While the early Christians posed only an evangelical threat to this accomplished life-style, it took the barbarians, who sacked the city in A.D. 476, to deal the fatal blow; what followed were hundreds of years in which Western Europe went unwashed.

A.D. 500–1075. Meanwhile, luxurious living had reached a zenith in the Eastern Roman Empire at Constantinople where a modified form of the Roman bath emerged. The Emperor Justinian I in A.D. 550, for example, saw to the completion of an ambitious system of conduits, fountains, and cisterns while the Dark Ages were already well-footed in the West. When the Eastern Roman Empire faced destruction in the eleventh century, its invaders, the Turks, were far more civilized than the Germanic hordes which had overrun the West.

Since the Seljuk Turks were already renowned for their *caravanserai*—oases built for bathing, resting, and feeding travelers—it should come as no surprise that the Turkish baths outshone even their Eastern Roman counterparts. Although these *caravanserai* also had warm rooms, hot rooms, and steam rooms, their intent—and by extension, their design—reflected a more relaxed philosophy of luxurious, recreational bathing than the baths of their Roman predecessors.

A.D. 1095–1500. Western Europe renewed

Charles Nes

its interest in bathing when the Crusaders imported the heathen habit they had embraced between battles in the Holy Land. Still, for the most part, Christendom endured the Middle Ages without any significant advances in plumbing and sanitation. In Britain, for example, feudal society was a subsistence one, preoccupied with surviving and the procuring of food and drink. Separate rooms for bathing and sleeping were virtually nonexistent. In the great halls of castles the servants slept communally around the fire. It was only the lord and lady who enjoyed the privacy of a bedchamber, which may or may not have been equipped with a sewage disposal chute opening directly into the castle moat.

Cleanliness at the table, however, did assume greater importance, since food still was eaten by hand. Predictably enough, the nobility were in the best position to elevate the standards of personal hygiene. With servants in attendance, washing the face, hands, and teeth at meals became something of a ritual accompanied by rose water, towels, and ornamental ewers. As the would-be ritual became

In the Chateau d'Blan Ville, tubs were placed against carved stone niches intended to contain the bath's warming vapor. Shell motif alludes to the mythological Poseidon.

Spa towns, which still function as major hydrotherapy establishments, have been assiduously frequented for their curative merits since antiquity. Under the auspices of Emperor Louis Napoleon and Empress Eugenie, spa towns became fully fledged places of fashionable resort. Competition between thermal establishments reached a zenith between 1880 and 1914 as French spas vied for customers with the German baden. In their Belle Epoque heyday, the French resorts were at the cutting edge of every fashion, whether medical, social, or architectural. Always trying to foster an up-to-the-minute image, they were furnished with the latest hydrotherapeutic and entertainment facilities. From initially modest and functional buildings there developed palatial thermal complexes dressed in a wonderfully eclectic range of styles. Full-blooded beaux arts classicism rubbed shoulders with the Byzantine or the Mauresque. The interiors were sumptuously decorated in tile, mosaic, and marbled polychromy. Hotels and casinos strove to match the splendor of the baths with their colonnaded promenades such as this one at Trinkhalle, which shaded the daily ritual of ablution and ingurgitation.

Charles Nes

more and more synonymous with fine breeding, it translated into a mandatory code of conduct which preceded every meal.

Bathing the entire body, however, was a different story. Since heating the water and filling the tub required considerable effort, bathing was not a common occurrence. When and if a tub was filled with hot water in a modest household, the entire family would gather to use the water; in a more prosperous household, the bath would most likely be more of a social activity accompanied by food and music.

Like beacons of civility, the monasteries throughout Europe managed to outwit the general squalor of the Middle Ages. Monks, unlike their secular contemporaries, slept in separate beds in rooms designed for that purpose. Baths were taken in the warm-water calefactory in wooden tubs padded with linen; routine washing before meals took place in a wash basin or laver.

Of course, it is necessary to look at the Middle Ages as a whole and understand that the improved standards of the nobility did set a standard for the masses, especially after what the Crusaders had witnessed in the East. By the end of the fourteenth century, Turkish baths were quite common in London and Paris, offering most people their first opportunity to bathe en masse since Roman times. Known as stews or bordellos, the baths soon became the favorite haunts of prostitutes. Once again the Church intervened, successfully closing the facilities in both France and England in the early sixteenth century.

Although the Church's action was justified on purely practical grounds—the baths were incubators for the plague and venereal disease—it does, nonetheless, characterize the prevailing attitude toward washing in the Middle Ages, for which the Church was largely responsible. To the churchmen of those times, Roman citizens' preoccupation with maintaining a clean and beautiful body represented the heathen's fatal pride; there was no true purity except that of the redeemed soul and the life hereafter, thus the medieval church taught its legions to reject the temporal and to have no faith in the earthly condition of man.

A.D. 1533–1603. During the reign of Elizabeth I of England during the following century, a gentleman by the name of Sir John Harrington published *A Metamorphosis of Ajax,* in which he

This vintage 1925 bath in the Manoir d'Ango combines cut stone, marble, and Italian mosaic tiles. Spanning the narrow width of the room, the extra-deep tub features a cutout side for easy access.

Charles Nes

included detailed plans for the lavatory bowl and valve-operated flushing system that he had installed in his own home. Little notice was taken so that even centuries later, the exemplary country houses of Elizabethan and Jacobean England still lacked sanitary and plumbing essentials. Householders all over Europe continued to empty their chamber pots from the windows, preceded only by the warning "Gardy-loo."

A.D. 1643–1800. The Court of King Louis XIV of France is almost universally credited with initiating a revolution in manners by which it led the known world in cultivated living. The finest furniture, painting, and crafts flourished amidst the unmatched splendor of Versailles. Strict rules governed dress and personal appearance, to the point where different styles of dress were as numerous as the ceremonial occasions for which they were required. The king's most basic domestic activities, such as rising and going to bed, were imbued with sanctity and converted into ceremony.

While the Age of Enlightenment ushered in heretofore unknown heights of ornamental beauty and literacy, standards of cleanliness were still all but medieval even among the few who practiced high etiquette. That is not to say that the era was completely devoid of a more civilized approach to the toilette. Money and craftsmanship now were lavished on giving ornamental beauty to the less glamorous aspects of everyday living. The close-stool or stool of ease, for example, replaced the garderobe, a stone or wooden seat above an open shaft. The stool was now a richly upholstered box with a hinged lid and padded seat inside of which was a removable vitreous pot. The Palace of Versailles boasted 264 such stools during the reign of Louis XIV, which at the very least was a testimony to the broadening attitude of the well-born French.

A.D. 1837–1901. It wasn't until well into the Victorian era that the pleasures of domestic comfort and interior decoration ceased to be a luxury and became a business. Many Victorians who prospered in the nineteenth century as a result of the Industrial Revolution were appalled at the conditions it had brought to the laboring masses. Manufacturing towns had brought congested misery to industrial centers. Minimal wages, intense poverty, and overcrowded tenements forced whole families

to share their beds. Bathtubs were almost unknown, epidemics commonplace, and gin was even safer to drink than water.

In the wealthy houses, however, domestic life was altogether different. Hot baths with liberal use of soap gradually replaced freezing douches, and bathrooms were serviced by armies of servants. The Victorian bedroom was cluttered with stylish bric-a-brac, chamber pots, bowl-and-jug sets, and tiled washstands.

While moral virtue was the great leveler of Victorian society, philanthropy and social reform became major preoccupations. Public hygiene now joined mandatory education and child labor as crusading issues. Parliament seriously turned its attention to public hygiene in the 1840s, when the buildup of sewage in the River Thames became unbearable. The building of public washhouses began in earnest now—admission price was a modest fee, and regular attendance was regarded as part of every working man's civic duty.

Designed by Le Corbusier in 1929, this bathroom at the Villa Savoye in Poissy, France is a forerunner of contemporary functionalism. Revealing the influential Swiss architect's view of interior spaces as either public or private cellular zones, the bathroom is actually a functional outgrowth of the bedroom. Contrasting shapes animate the space, while the tile surface and built-in chaise suggest the health-giving virtues of sun, air, and cleanliness. The slablike wardrobe at left anchors the curtain rod and partitions the bath area from an access corridor and the bedroom.

Bathhouses and hydrotherapy resorts flourished in America at the turn of the century. The Palace Bathhouse in Eureka Springs, Arkansas—washed in the honky-tonk light of its red neon sign—is an outstanding example that still exists today.

Richard Johnson

The morally concerned Victorian attitude saw washing as the baptism through which the common man had to pass before he could improve his social condition, his mind, and ultimately save his soul. Cleanliness rather than squalor was the prerequisite for salvation.

One would still be hard-pressed to prove that cleanliness was widespread at that time. As late as the 1860s, New York's best hotels still only provided water for washing hands and face. Townspeople and farmers alike patronized outhouses. Privies in the rear of the backyard were standard in even large and expensive houses until the 1840s. At about that time, Simon Baruch, father of Bernard Baruch the statesman, zealously campaigned for public baths. His dream came to fruition a full ten years later with the opening of New York's first People's Baths, a portent of the future.

A.D. 1901–Present. In contrast to his predecessors, twentieth-century man believes himself to be the most ideally clean of creatures. Virtually all house design today—at least in the Western democracies—is built around a central utility core that carries all the essential plumbing necessities. Improved technology and techniques of mass production played an increasingly important role in domestic life; 1910 saw the first cheap manufacture of cast-iron enameled bathtubs. But the catalysts for drastic adaptations in domestic life were provided by the two world wars. Technological development was given a significant boost, and deodorization became a twentieth-century cleansing phenomenon, fueled by shrewd advertising and human insecurity.

Hollywood did much to heighten the concept of the bath as a luxury retreat. Producers and directors

Designer Melanie Kahane created this luxurious bathroom for showman Billy Rose more than thirty years ago. Located in Rose's famous Carnegie Hill mansion in New York City, the bathroom demonstrates Ms. Kahane's skill for enduring style. Doubling as a small salon, the room features hand-carved **boiserie** paneling, silk-covered furnishings, antique needlepoint carpet, and a fine-cut crystal chandelier. Although Kahane redecorated the mansion through two of Rose's subsequent marriages, this room remained untouched, as it was one of his favorites.

Bath House Row in Hot Springs, Arkansas is lined with some of this country's most famous spas. Although the ravages of time have left their interiors in a state of surreal neglect, one can easily imagine the luxury that prevailed in years gone by. (Left) *At the Fordyce Bathhouse, a crumbling partition announces an old-fashioned steam bath.* (Right) *Down the hall, forgotten massage tables stand with guarded symmetry.*

Richard Johnson

(Right) *Marilyn Monroe luxuriates in a freestanding tub in* **The Seven Year Itch.** (Below) *In* **One Week,** *the 1920 Metro film, Buster Keaton is featured in a less-than-luxurious bathroom.* (Far right) *Rosalind Russell, at left, and Joan Crawford, at right, exemplify the heightened awareness of the bath as a self-contained luxury retreat in* **The Women,** *a 1939 Metro-Goldwyn-Mayer picture.*

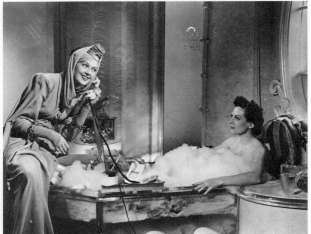

The Museum of Modern Art/Film Stills Archive

soon discovered that sexploitation accompanied by lush settings made for box-office hits—and where moviemakers trod, manufacturers were soon to follow. Cecil B. DeMille discovered the bathroom as a viable screen device when in *Male and Female* he discreetly lingered over the disrobing Gloria Swanson and, in the process, brought bathing out into the open. Despite a repertoire of seduction locales ranging from volcanoes to submarines, the screen bathroom still managed to provide a handy new vehicle for James Bond (Sean Connery) in *Diamonds Are Forever.* Jill St. John succumbed to 007's charms in a huge, round acrylic tub, the ledge of which was filled with tropical fish and fauna.

With standards of domestic comfort at an all-time high, today's bathroom can offer the sybarite every opportunity for indulgence. The bath can now be enjoyed as an acceptable domestic retreat in most households and as such has undergone a metamorphosis. The fitness craze is, of course, partially responsible for reconceptualizing and repositioning the bath. In addition to its most basic functions, the bath must now ameliorate the escalating stresses of everyday life. Saunas, whirlpools,

and exercise equipment imbue today's bath with a new sporting outlook. Audio and video components are no longer restricted to media rooms and are helping to redefine our ideas of luxury and privacy.

Despite these facts, bathrooms are not always all they can and should be. Rather than constituting a testing ground for imaginative design exploration, bath design can all too often result in bland, uninviting interiors. But the issue is more than just one of alternative interiors—any competent architect or interior designer can make intelligent cabinetry and finish choices and can ensure that lighting and plumbing are at requisite levels and conveniently situated. More important than the completion of a task or a problem neatly solved is the attempt to push beyond such planning rudiments—to embrace a new modernism that enhances rather than obscures the relationship between design and humanity. The new modernism should respond to basic human needs with function and character. If the Bauhaus virtue of "form follows function" continues as a guiding light, then perhaps fixtures and bath devices will become more ergonomically sensible without compromising their design integrity.

As part of a project funded by American Standard, a group of senior students from the Art Center College of Design at Pasadena, California created a series of experimental baths. (Left) *Harry Howard, Juan Montesa, Russ Rucker, and Steve Yagian created this open-style bath with ergonomically molded fixtures of their own design.* (Above) *This single-column design by Sally Hadler and Joan Sunol acts as a washbasin, shower, and w.c. unit.*

DESIGN
PORTFOLIO

TRADITIONAL

The roots of the traditional style lie in eighteenth-century Europe—in the manor houses of England, the châteaux of France, and the palazzi of Italy. The reigning monarchs and favored aristocracy collectively advanced furniture-making skills and interior design with their appetite for luxury and comfort. As their preferences continued to dictate prevailing style, major periods assumed the appropriate monarch's name, ruling dynasty, or even type of government. With such noble patronage, traditional style developed from early crude and clumsy attempts to make life a little easier and more secure to the incredible ornamental achievements of the French rococo style. Yet other design movements were brewing outside the influential aristocratic circles. Country and provincial styles, for example, were colonial interpretations that descended from traditional influences. In some cases, the basic designs used were copies, with the differences resulting from cruder tools and limited skills. In others, colonial craftsmen used plain, simple ornamentation native to their localities or injected their own decorative ideas. In every instance, however, the provincial designs were less ornate and sophisticated.

Rooms decorated in the traditional style are intended for comfort and imbued with a sense of heritage. Decorated according to period canons of taste, they seek to combine the essence of historical integrity with picturesque effect. Applied ornamentation in the form of carpeting, rich upholstery, and draperies enhances the elegant introspection characteristic of traditional spaces. The intrinsic patina of age is enhanced by layers of mementos and heirlooms; fine silver, crystal, ivory, and even wood marquetry demonstrate the artistic personality of the age as well as of the collector inhabitant. Architectural detailing strengthens the link to the past while providing surface dimension and structural significance.

Yet the major decorative movements have always run in cycles—their designs and general characteristics selectively revived throughout the ages. Although this phenomenon is as old as culture itself, such artistic reviviscence also signals vibrant aesthetic health. A "new traditionalism" is currently making its mark as a favored and more livable design scheme. It is essentially lighter in feeling, with furnishings pulled mainly from the neoclassic styles. Crisper, lighter fabrics replace the old velvets and brocades, while fruitwood replaces the darker, more oppressive walnut and mahogany. This currently renewed interest in traditionalism—albeit a new traditionalism—is significant: While reaffirming the style's wide appeal, it also demonstrates our perenially ambivalent connection with history and, at the same time, nourishes our modern sensibility with new directions and themes.

Dennis Krukowshi/Southampton Designers Showcase

DESIGNER
JOHN ROBERT MOORE

In this small Southhampton, New York, bathroom, designer John Robert Moore used decorative sleight-of-hand for romantic effect.

Moore enlivened the space, tucked away in a formerly dark corner of the house's upper story, with a pastel wallcovering in a buttoned cushion motif. A hand-painted marbleized finish on the rolled steel tub and a gathered chintz skirt on the washbasin make refreshing, if unlikely, companions.

Selected accessories include a ribbon-hung eighteenth-century oil painting and a gilt-framed Irish mirror, c. 1825. A double-arm, wall-mounted sconce with frosted glass shades illuminates.

A very fine antique needlepoint carpet sets a garden motif under a *faux* bamboo regency baby chair that recalls a stately era.

DESIGNER

CHARLES KREWSON

Setting aside a program of structural alterations, designer Charles Krewson enhanced the character of this prewar bath with a personal collection of silver and ivory accessories and fine art photography. Working in a palette of black and white, Krewson's zebra-striped towels and seat cover keep the two-color mix from becoming too earnest.

Taking his cues from the black-and-white ceramic cross-weave floor treatment and tile dado, Krewson glazed the walls jet black. A collection of photographs by Cecil Beaton and Hoyningen-Huene echo the palette and decorate both the walls and three-panel folding screen.

A small marble and wrought-iron garden table is the mainstay for a collection of cut glass, silver, and inlaid boxes—which provide additional sources of texture and gleam in the room. Lighting is by way of a wall sconce over the seventeenth-century Dutch picture frame turned medicine cabinet.

Collectibles add history and character to the grooming area. A Chinese celadon porcelain vase (c. 1914) presides over Indian **Bidri** *silver inlay lead boxes and* **Bidri** *cup, Seiko talking pyramid clock, and cut-glass perfume bottles from Aspreys. Lily-pad silver tray (c. 1900), Christofle; silver on sink, Tiffany; ivory accessories, Floris, London.*

Dennis Krukowski

Painted faux bois cabinetry combines eighteenth-century style with contemporary storage needs. Decorative furnishings include spindle chair and small, carved étagère. Bath fixtures and fittings, American Standard; carpeting, Stark; wallcovering, Brunschwig & Fils.

George Cserna

D E S I G N E R
DENNIS ROLLAND

Figured cabinetry answers the need for additional storage in this bath designed by Dennis Rolland. The authentic-looking burled elm woodwork actually sports a convincing *faux bois* finish by artist Graham Smith.

Capitalizing on the unused space above the washbasin, Rolland designed a self-contained grooming niche consisting of a storage pier, grooming mirror, light sconce, and vanity. There is even a plate rail to display a collection of porcelain dinner-

ware. Panel-molding details and brass hardware enhance the eighteenth-century period styling.

An obliquely angled storage vanity features a white marble counter with splashboard and extension ledge over the w.c. An oval unrimmed washbasin is served by brass-plated spread-set fittings in period style. Treated as a panel detail, the mirror over the counter features its own *faux bois* molded frame.

Fringed shower curtains are an unexpected detail more commonly encountered as parlor window treatments. A Victorian side chair holds towels while the wall-mounted étagère displays toiletries. A contemporary carpet adds a lively geometric motif beneath a Chinese-style, antique toile lantern.

Jaime Ardiles Arce

(Above) *Tent-flap window treatment is attached to walls with steel industrial grommets. Oversized three-foot-by-seven-foot stainless steel tub, washbasin and quarry-stone table are custom designs. Walls are marbleized in a trompe l'oeil rustication. Ruined column features revolving center sections for storage.*

(Left) *Custom-designed carpet features a burgundy border that dictates the placement of furnishings. The adjoining master bedroom in the background features a custom-designed sleigh bed with gessoed frame.*

D E S I G N E R
JOHN DICKENSON

Designer John Dickenson brings a strong sense of the past, especially the classical past, to his work. His trademarks abound but never overwhelm.

Conjuring up a contemporary Pompeian fantasy, the walls and ceiling are covered in a subtle marbleized rustication. A large, custom-design stainless steel tub dominates the room, conveying both sparseness and precision. This oversized three-foot-by-seven-foot tub features wide rolled edges and mitered and welded corners. Plumbing was also carefully arranged so that hot water runs through pipes under the tub, through a freestanding brass towel rail and then into the tub itself. This maneuver preheats the tub and helps maintain the water temperature inside for more comfortable bathing.

Custom-designed water controls simulate gold nuggets and are mounted on the longest side of the tub. A simple hole in its side replaces the more conventional spout.

The vanity is a molded and bent block of stainless steel with an integrated washbasin. The same gold nugget taps are repeated here. Symmetrically placed windows flank the sink and are covered with roll-up shades marbleized to match the walls. Above them are canvas tent flaps fastened to the wall with steel grommets.

Appointments include the carved mirror and goat-foot table beside the tub, both designed by Dickenson. A simulated ruined column in the corner features revolving center sections for storage. Floor treatment is gray carpeting, with a burgundy border encircling the tub and running around the perimeter of the room.

Lighting is by way of recessed floods and a brass pharmacy lamp beside the tub.

Black Tizio lamp presides over a vignette of personal grooming accessories. Bird's-eye maple drum table and chaise lounge are both custom designs by John Saladino. Window blind, Levolor.

D E S I G N E R
JOHN SALADINO

Designed by John Saladino, this spacious bath/ sitting room invites emotional as well as physical ablution. Romantic lighting, pastel coloration, and artful furnishings lend a tranquil note against a backdrop of traditional architectural detailing.

Existing architectural features were restored and given new surface treatments—the mantel was bleached and pickled while the ceiling cornice was glazed and the marble surround was restored. The original wood-plank floor was replaced with a treatment of two-inch-square tile in a matte finish.

A heavy porcelain bathtub from the twenties was set atop a bleached oak plinth in the center of the room. With a glass-topped and columned side table, the tub looks more like a comfortable seating element than a cleansing or therapeutic amenity. Hovering over the tub is a large brass-plated punkah—or Indian fan. Motion is activated by a mechanical engine with cable and wheel mounted on a pickled wood column.

A mechanical wheel and cable for the punkah are mounted on an eighteenth-century English wine cooler styled as a classic column. Custom-designed drum table illuminates the antique tapestry-clad folding screen. Floor treatment is pink ceramic tile. Tile, American Olean.

All furnishings were designed by John Saladino and include a post-and-beam sofa with an ash frame and terry-covered cushions, as well as an ash chaise. Objects arranged in still-life fashion include: capitals over the mantel, tabletop vignettes of sponges and brushes, a doctor's scale, and even the folding screen.

Lighting in the room is arranged for effect and mood. Floor to ceiling silk panels mounted behind the cornice can be slid over the windows to control the light, while matchstick shades further diffuse the exposure. For evening illumination, the panels are back-lit along the perimeter floor line. Ceiling-mounted pinspots highlight individual objects.

Bleached wood plinth elevates old-fashioned tub to center stage. Georgian-style chimneypiece is surmounted by four architectural capitals, while over the tub, a large brass punkah—an Indian ceiling fan—presides.

Dan Eifert

(Right) *Victorian chest with burnt-bamboo trim and eighteenth-century botanicals in burled-elm frames mitigate the monastic spirit of the w.c. Natural light streaks through narrow glass-block slit. Wallcovering is subtle blue-and-white stripe. Victorian chest, botanical prints, Objets Plus.*

(Far right) *A wall of figured mirror cabinetry provides wardrobe storage in the dressing corridor. Glass-block wall, platform whirlpool tub and vanity are reflected. Open door leads to separate w.c. Floor treatment is travertine marble. Lighting consists of recessed floods with polished steel collars.*

D E S I G N E R

RUBÉN DE SAAVEDRA

With this combination dressing room/bath, designer Rubén de Saavedra reinstates the boudoir to its eighteenth-century position of domestic prominence and elegance. A palette of cool surface treatments is warmed by a selection of fine antique furnishings and accessories.

Located in a large New York City penthouse, the two-room suite incorporates a full range of bath conveniences along with considerable wardrobe storage behind a wall of figured mirror cabinetry.

An entire wall of glass block ensures privacy yet provides daylight for the person using the platform-mounted whirlpool tub. The platform deck and access steps are clad in travertine marble to match

the floor treatment throughout. A mirrored étagère at the head of the tub also provides convenient towel storage. Additional lighting is provided by recessed floodlights with polished steel collars.

A combination dressing table/vanity occupies the wall alongside the whirlpool tub. Fitted with an unrimmed oval washbasin and travertine marble top, the table is a practical adornment. Shallow makeup drawers over the kneehole and a built-in clothes hamper complement the more inventive zinc-lined drawer for hot rollers and the adjustable, slide-out television shelf. Behind the dressing table, a polished steel, swing-arm vanity mirror augments the mirrored medicine cabinet.

With architectural sleight-of-hand, de Saavedra concealed the w.c. in its own "closet." The small, functional space features a stripe wallcovering and is appointed with a Victorian chest that has a top-mounted vanity mirror and burnt-bamboo trim. On the wall, a pair of fine eighteenth-century botanicals in burled-elm frames presides, while a narrow glass-block window diffuses ambient light.

Two marble-clad steps access the platform-mounted whirlpool tub. Combination vanity/dressing table is fitted with unrimmed oval washbasin. Louis XVI-style swivel chair presides. Glass-block wall borrows light and ensures privacy. Whirlpool tub, washbasin, fittings, American Standard.

Peter Vitale

Frank Ritter

Clear glass panels and brass trim frame the entry to this fantasy bathroom. A surface treatment of inlaid seashells in a diamond-panel motif covers the walls and floor; a simpler shell application appears on the ceiling and vanity as well. Ceiling-mounted pinspots dramatically highlight selected objects.

DESIGNER
FRED PALATINUS

Designer Fred Palatinus used inlaid seashells on the walls, floor, and ceiling for this opulent, one-of-a-kind bathroom. The diamond-panel motif and coffered ceiling bring classical architectural spirit to Palatinus's unusual design application.

A cantilevered vanity shelf fitted with an oval brass washbasin runs along the left side of the room. The commodious shelf provides ample space for toiletries, as well as for large shell urns with orchid plants. Over the vanity is a wide-frame pediment mirror, while underneath it a copper leather-covered stool provides convenient seating.

A brass-trimmed partition beside the vanity architecturally signals the w.c. and bidet. Both are located on the other side of the partition behind a bronze mirror door.

A low-stepped platform is fitted with a sunken brass tub custom designed by Palatinus. A second stool, covered in the same copper-colored leather, holds towels at the foot of the tub.

Furnishings throughout the space continue the glittering opulence. A small glass-and-steel *guéridon* is flanked by an Empire-style armchair and brass-and-glass vitrine. At the center of the space is a leather-covered daybed and low Chinese lacquered table.

A single ceiling-mounted etched-glass lantern provides ambient illumination, while a series of low-voltage pinspots dramatically highlight objects furnishings, textures, and patterns.

DESIGNER
RONALD BRICKE

Designer Ronald Bricke reconciles the classic origins of this powder room with a mixed palette of contemporary surface treatments. A marble checkerboard floor treatment, trompe l'oeil inlaid dado, and stenciled cornice have been successfully fused for both artistic and decorative effect.

An existing porcelain washbasin with a fluted-column pedestal sets the classical tone for this small powder room. Original fittings were replaced with a pewter-and-ivory handled set. The custom-designed medicine cabinet over the washbasin continues the classical theme with oversized, mitered corner moldings top and bottom. The unit also features a built-in light trough and mirror for task situations.

A marbleized trompe l'oeil dado painted by Crista relieves the all-gray walls. Its diamond-inlay motif of gray and beige marble is somewhat repeated in the diagonal checkerboard marble floor treatment. A wavelike stenciled cornice clarifies the ceiling height, while an existing window niche sports swagged silk curtains.

An oak towel rail occupies the niche by the window, and an alabaster lamp lights the room.

Richard Barnes

Marbleized trompe l'oeil dado, stenciled cornice, and pedestal-column washbasin lend classical ambience to this small powder room. Custom medicine cabinet features oversized corner moldings and built-in light. Antique alabaster ceiling fixture illuminates. W.c., American Standard; fittings, P.E. Guerin; antique alabaster lamp, Marvin Alexander.

The rolled-steel tub and fitted lead shower were purchased in a Paris flea market. Wallcovering of mottled parchment squares adds subtle surface interest. Carved and painted Blackamoor table between settee and washbasin holds candlestick lamp. "Parentesi" floor lamp, Atelier International.

Peter Bosch

DESIGNER
TIM ROMANELLO

For this gentlemen's bath/sitting room, designer Tim Romanello successfully manages austerity with period elegance. Antique bath essentials share the space with comfortable seating in a room that often doubles for intimate entertaining.

A lucky find at a Paris flea market, an antique rolled-steel tub with fitted lead shower is the room's focal point. Brass finials, water controls, and return pipes highlight the shower with a kind of gilded elegance, making it unusually compatible with the rest of the antique furnishings. A porcelain washbasin with fluted-column pedestal completes the amenities profile.

A Napoleon III settee and club chair provide intimate seating in a far corner. Antique Turkish carpets, finished with oversized rope welting and fringe, are an unusual upholstery treatment. The mahogany *bibliothèque* holds a small library along with a candlestick lamp and casually propped etching.

Mottled parchment wallcovering adds subtle surface interest and provides a complementary backdrop for the collection of eighteenth-century oils in gilded frames. Lighting is provided by recessed floods, several candlestick lamps, and a cable-mounted floor lamp. Floorcovering is sisal matting.

Napoleon III settee and club chair are covered in Turkish carpets with rope welting and fringe. Mahogany bibliothèque displays vignette of treasured mementos. Floorcovering is sisal matting, table is African.

Dan Eifert

(Top) *Regency wall sconce and gilt-framed etching add period elegance. Swing-arm wall lamp illuminates for reading. Whirlpool, Hastings Tile & Il Bagno Collection; swing-arm lamp, Hansen.*

(Right) *Brass washbasin and polished-steel fittings convert Irish mask table into vanity. Custom-designed mirror features chipped-amber glass frame. Red-lacquer tray holds towels. Washbasin, fittings, Paul Associates; towels, Halston.*

DESIGNERS
ZAJAC & CALLAHAN

An eighteenth-century oak console table, *bronze-doré* wall sconces, and chipped glass mirror lend sitting-room elegance to this bathroom designed by Edward Zajac and Richard Callahan. Juxtaposed against a backdrop of upholstered strie walls, the ensemble is completed by contemporary Italian bath fixtures in white porcelain.

The approach successfully maintains decorative compatibility with an adjoining guestroom.

A fine eighteenth-century Irish mask console table was reincarnated as an elegant vanity with an oval, brass washbasin and polished steel fittings. A note of glittering elegance is lent by the custom-design mirror with chipped-amber glass frame. A wall-mounted swing-arm lamp with brass shade illuminates the vignette.

A self-rimming whirlpool tub sits beside the vanity completely enclosed by upholstered panels with nail-head trim. Water controls, whirlpool, and flexible shower hose are mounted on the deck along the side, while a molded headrest is at the head of the tub. The companion w.c. sits in a preexisting wall niche by the entry.

A simple window treatment features double-hung fabric panels topped by a lambrequin trimmed in brass nail-heads. A matchstick shade diffuses light.

Immediately beneath the window is a leopard-covered regency baby chair; on either side, a pair of very fine regency wall sconces.

Wallcovering, curtains, and tub enclosure are all of the same ivory-and-beige cotton strie fabric.

Newly fitted washbasin converts an eighteenth-century Italian console table into a vanity. Small folding screen holds paper towels and conceals w.c. on the other side. Floorcovering is beige-and-black terrazzo marble with contrasting diamond motif and edge trim.

DESIGNERS

DENNING & FOURCADE

The height of old-world elegance best describes this bathroom, designed by Robert Denning and Vincent Fourcade. A backdrop of beige terrazzo marble and mirror panels sets off an ensemble of fine antiques and rare objects that successfully captures the glamour of a bygone era.

An existing pilastered mantel architecturally divides the space into two distinct areas, with washbasin, shower stall, and w.c. on one side and bathtub on the other. Placed slightly off center left, a carved and painted eighteenth-century console table is reincarnated as a vanity with a newly fitted washbasin; placing the sink slightly off-center leaves most of the marble top free for storage and display. The w.c. is inventively hidden behind the panels of a folding screen. Immediately opposite, an obliquely angled shower stall features a polished-steel and clear-glass enclosure.

Beige terrazzo marble wall and floor treatment features a neo-Italian contrasting black diamond motif and edge trim. Ambient illumination is from an overhead French crystal chandelier and pair of ormolu-and-bronze mounted regency candelabra.

At the sink, a brass picture light enhances a classical mural and facilitates grooming. A mirror-tiled ceiling heightens the room's glamour, while mirrored wall panels expand the space.

Lizzie Himmel/Southampton Designers Showcase

D E S I G N E R
TOM O'TOOLE

Designer Tom O'Toole used checkerboard-tiled dado, mattress-ticking wall treatment, and a converted sideboard vanity to update this traditional gentlemen's bathroom. Located in the eaves of a large Southampton, New York, house, the newly renovated space is both inviting and elegant.

Set in its own mirrored niche, a triple-drawer Welsh sideboard doubles as a vanity with a newly fitted brass washbasin. Brass-plated hospital fittings from Kraft feature a gooseneck spout and winged lever controls. A brass swing-arm light fixture with a pleated silk shade and an eighteenth-century botanical complete the vignette.

The separate bath area occupies the space between an existing window and architectural wall jag. A mirror-faced platform with oak deck encloses a white oval whirlpool tub. Mounted on the window side of the tub, period-style brass-plated fittings incorporate water controls, diverter, and flexible hand-held shower head.

An ocean liner deck chair replaces the conventional upholstered chaise, while an antique cotton Agra carpet enlivens the stained-oak floor.

(Above) *An oval brass washbasin converts an antique Welsh sideboard into a stylish vanity. Brass-plated hospital fittings are an unexpected gesture. Brass swing-arm lamp, eighteenth-century botanical, and mirror panels complete the vignette. Washbasin and fittings, Kraft.*

(Left) *Oval whirlpool tub is enclosed in a mirror-faced platform with oak deck. Dual wall treatment combines checkerboard-tile dado and mattress-ticking wallcovering. Ocean liner deck chair replaces more conventional upholstered chaise. Tile, whirlpool tub, Hastings Tile & Il Bagno Collection; silkscreen prints, Howard Hodgkins; carpet, Stark.*

A sculpted onyx pedestal washbasin and w.c. fuse luxury and practicality. Metallic-silk upholstered walls set off gilt-framed mirror, light-box fixture, and architectural engravings. Carpeting features leopard-spot motif. All bathroom fixtures and fittings, including mirror, light and soapdish, Sherle Wagner; fabric, Yves Gonnet; carpet, Stark.

Phillip Ennis

D E S I G N E R S

MARSHALL - SCHULE ASSOCIATES

Silk-covered walls and precious materials establish the jewel-box quality of this powder room, designed by Ned Marshall and Harry Schule.

Taking center stage as functional sculpture is an onyx pedestal vanity fitted with twenty-four-karat gold-plated washbasin and fittings. A companion w.c., carved from two matching solid blocks of onyx, features a white porcelain inset bowl and twenty-four-karat gilt seat cover.

Gilt-framed mirror and light box over the vanity facilitate grooming, as does the wall-mounted crystal soapdish. Three fine architectural engravings lend an air of artistic restraint amid the opulence.

Padded and upholstered walls invite the obvious jewel-box analogy. The same metallic silk on the walls and ceiling is also used for the tieback shower curtains. Carpeting features a suitably elegant leopard-spot motif that reiterates swirling patterns of the pedestal vanity and w.c.

Traditional millwork is evident in the hand-carved dado, window frame and reveal, and ceiling cornice. Unusual vertical light strip with brass and frosted-glass inset panels adjoins the mirrored wall. Overhead lantern features etched-glass shade mounted in bronze.

DESIGN
SONNENBERG MANSION

Traditional appointments relieve the austere red-and-black palette of this powder room located in New York's historic Sonnenberg Mansion.

Hand-carved dado with traditional panel-molding detail encloses the space on all four sides. A small black-lacquered vanity is fitted with a gray marble top finished with radius corners. An un-rimmed oval washbasin is served by three solid-brass fittings. On the tank of the w.c., a brass-trimmed marble slab doubles as a convenience and display ledge.

For added spaciousness, the entire wall behind the vanity is mirrored from the top of the dado to the ceiling. A deep-set window with carved reveal and frame, corner étagère with porcelain tea set, and mahogany oval mirror in reflection relieve the otherwise all-red wall treatment. A black lacquered crown molding clarifies the ceiling line.

An unusual custom-designed light strip in brass and frosted glass is corner-mounted between the mirror and window wall. Lighting is provided by a ceiling-mounted etched-glass and bronze lantern.

Norman McGrath

Wainscot paneling on the walls and tub enclosure complement the barroom elegance of an etched-glass pub mirror. Rolled-brass handrail, tub fittings, and brass soapdish accessorize with period charm. Portable television stands atop antique step chest.

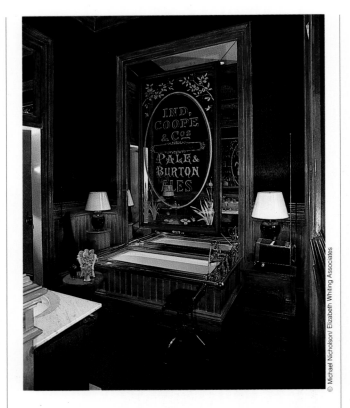

© Michael Nicholson/ Elizabeth Whiting Associates

D E S I G N E R
JOHN DICKENSON

Mahogany millwork, black upholstered walls, and an etched-glass pub mirror lend the ambience of a private barroom to designer John Dickenson's bathroom. Located in the designer's converted firehouse residence, the now-cozy space often doubles as a television/reading room.

Wainscot paneling on the walls and tub enclosure lends a tone of casual yet masculine elegance. Immediately behind the tub, an antique etched-glass pub mirror advertises Pale & Burton Ales with commanding understatement. The rolled-brass handrail, tub fittings, and brass soapdish all enhance the publike feeling.

A black upholstered wallcovering and dark carpeting keep the room intimate, while a dropped crown molding scales the ceiling to a more manageable height.

Mood lighting comes from a pair of ginger-jar lamps flanking the tub atop cylindrical storage pedestals. An antique step chest doubles as a perch for the small portable television.

D E S I G N E R S
KEMP & SIMMERS

Designing a storage-system for a collection of first editions and current best-sellers, designers Friederike Kemp Biggs and Jean P. Simmers turned this seldom-used powder room into a multifunctional library.

Located in the upper story of a Southampton, New York, mansion, the original millwork features a coat of slate-colored paint, while the walls are enlivened with a paisleylike, marbleized paper. A cantilevered shelf with a fitted washbasin occupies the existing wall niche and permits additional book storage below.

A system of brass-trimmed shelves lines the walls from the top of the painted dado to the ceiling. The brass-studded library ladder affords access to the uppermost shelves, while the triangular mahogany sewing table makes a convenient perch for books in progress.

The existing w.c. was treated to a marbleized trompe l'oeil finish for an added touch of whimsical fantasy. Wall-mounted sconce beside the window is brass with a white pleated-linen shade.

In this unusual bathroom, the designers have managed to successfully revive the traditional study and embellish it with the modern device of *faux* finishes. Since the room is rather narrow, attention is drawn to the window that visually opens up the space and provides a frame for decorative objects.

Brass-trimmed shelves and window niche hold a collection of first editions. A trompe l'oeil w.c. in a marbleized finish faces a niche-mounted vanity. Brass-studded library ladder completes the look, while the sisal-covered floor adds a note of casual informality.

Phillip Ennis

(Right) *An angled beam bisects the shower enclosure and anchors the cantilevered double vanity. Enlarged skylights and recessed floods enhance the uneven tones of the tiles. All bathroom fittings and fixtures, American Standard; tile, Marble Technics.*

(Below) *Set atop its own obliquely angled platform, the self-rimming whirlpool looks through floor-to-ceiling doors. Marble-topped vanity features open shelves for towel storage. Whirlpool, American Standard.*

ARCHITECTURAL DESIGNERS
FLORENCE PERCHUK, LIVIO DIMITRIU, & CARL SAMOL

INTERIOR DESIGNER
MARY DIAL

Architectural designers Florence Perchuk, Livio Dimitriu, and Carl Samol created this four-hundred-square-foot bathroom by combining two former baths with a former storage space. Enter interior designer Mary Dial who embellished the space with sleek bath fixtures, fossilized stone tile, and stained structural beams.

Architectural modifications set the stage for two distinct bath and grooming zones: the shower room—with a tiled kiosk enclosure, double vanity, w.c., and bidet—and a separate dressing room—with whirlpool bath, additional washbasin, and w.c.

The tiled shower cylinder dominates the first room. Pierced by two openings and an angled beam, the enclosure features a raised basin line for water control and a built-in corner ledge and soap niche. The tile treatment throughout precludes the need for any splashboards.

A cantilevered double vanity wraps around the same angled beam off the opposite wall. Each trapezoidal-shaped end is paved with the same tile as the floor and walls and fitted with individual self-rimming washbasins. Mirror panels over the vanity are topped by a continuous light bridge fitted into the notched half-cylinder above, which doubles as a medicine cabinet.

At the far end of the space, a mullioned door frame and transom define the dressing room, which is appointed with platform-mounted whirlpool, additional washbasin, vanity, and w.c.

Fossilized limestone tile is used throughout as a surface treatment on the walls, floors, and counter-tops. The eight-inch-square tiles were cut on the job to fit the various conditions that each area required.

Porcelainized steel tub with rolled rim and ball-and-claw feet sports new coat of regency red paint. Towels are inscribed with the designer's initials, JVP. Pair of eighteenth-century prints, private collection; w.c., American Standard; towels, Leron.

Original turn-of-the-century washbasin is skirted to match the wallcovering. Eighteenth-century dressing table displays cut-crystal objects, while **faux** *bamboo chair complements. Silver-leafed mirror reflects wall sconce and four stylized equestrian prints.*

DESIGNER
JOSEF PRICCI

Rich colors, period furnishings, and stylized equestrian prints lend sporting elegance to this country bath designed by Josef Pricci. The room's casual outlook refreshingly belies its Southampton, New York, estate location.

The surprise regency red painted floor and wainscoting visually anchor the delicate motif of the wallcovering. An elevated chair rail architecturally fuses the dual wall treatment and scales the ceiling to a more manageable height.

Original fixtures were both renewed and replaced: The existing turn-of-the-century marble vanity is skirted to match the wallcovering, while the porcelainized steel tub with ball-and-claw feet sports a new exterior coat of red paint. A simple white porcelain w.c. replaces the original.

The long wall opposite the tub allowed Pricci to accessorize for both comfort and effect. A mahogany dressing table and companion *faux* bamboo chair enjoy newfound prominence. A nineteenth-century library lamp with pleated silk shade illuminates the tabletop vignette, including silver Art Nouveau mirror, picture frame, silver-mounted perfume flasks, and cigarette boxes.

Walls over the dressing table and tub showcase four stylized horse prints and a pair of eighteenth-century landscapes respectively. At the vanity, a silver-leafed mirror and wall sconce preside.

(Right) *Pedestal washbasin is flanked by Victorian conversation chair and triple-tier étagère. Wallpaper borders are used as ceiling frieze and over chair rail. Wall-hung photographs feature trompe l'oeil beribboned frames painted by Neas. Pedestal washbasin, fittings, Sherle Wagner.*

(Far right) *Silk taffeta curtains frame bay window and tub niche. Folding screen conceals w.c., while mahogany* bibliothèque *doubles for towel storage and as dressing table. A* faux marbre *floor treatment painted by the designer completes the room. All fabrics and wallcoverings, Brunschwig & Fils.*

D E S I G N E R
RICHARD LOWELL NEAS

Designer Richard Lowell Neas captures the elegance of a bygone era in this turn-of-the-century bathroom. Dark mahogany antiques, *faux marbre* floor treatment, and elaborate wallpaper borders authentically recall the style of an Edwardian gentleman.

Plaid silk taffeta curtains frame the newly created bathing niche and antique rolled-steel tub. White opaque curtains hung cafe-style ensure privacy, while a carved and inlaid Moroccan side table lends ethnic flavor. To one side of the niche, a fabric-covered folding screen hides the w.c., while a white pedestal washbasin balances the symmetry.

Appointments on this side of the room include a pair of swing-arm lamps fitted with woven shades and a Gothic-style vanity mirror. An antique Victorian conversation chair with leopard-motif upholstery and a three-tiered étagère complete the grooming area of the bath. A comfortable Empire chaise lounge with gilt animal paws invites relaxing moments.

Surface treatments include the *faux marbre* finish on the floor painted by the designer, as well as the patterned wallcovering, scalloped wallpaper valance, and double-bordered chair rail.

A wall treatment of "calculated urban decay" sets off an ensemble of idiosyncratic artifacts. Hand-carved Italian mirror combines five period styles alongside an American kerosene lamp. Closely cropped portrait was painted by owner, Robert Drew.

Dan Eifert

D E S I G N E R
ROBERT DREW

In his own bathroom, drawing instructor and artist Robert Drew elevates calculated neglect to a fine art. Peeling and corroded walls are appreciated for their intrinsic color and texture, much like those of a timeworn European villa. And it is against such a background that an ensemble of questionable pedigree assumes commanding artistic value.

What makes this interior so special is that rare fruition of attitude and artifact—conventional pedigree is of little or no interest to Drew. Instead objects are selected for their idiosyncratic charm or wit.

The hand-carved Italian mirror over the w.c., for example, is an amalgam of five period styles, including Louis XIV, XV, and XVI, as well as the Empire eagle and Directoire farm implements. The wall-mounted American kerosene is circa "Third Avenue Junk," while behind it the soulful face of a Drew portrait presides. Nearby, a bronze figure on the w.c. tank quietly maintains her dignity.

DESIGNER
JOHN SALADINO

A vaulted ceiling and painted walls recall the faded glory of Pompeii in this bathroom designed by John Saladino. Located in a newly renovated penthouse, the space successfully blends contemporary needs and classical yearnings.

Trompe l'oeil artist David Fisch used a classical Roman palette of earth pigments to recall the patched frescoes and benign neglect of a Pompeian grotto. Rectangular painted wall panels in a concentric motif are surmounted by smaller panels depicting scenes of Cupid borne by sea serpents and Cupid carting baskets of flowers. The architecturally vaulted ceiling was painted with symmetrical coffers, while the Roman-style grille over the washbasin and the radiator enclosure were both covered in oxidized copper leaf.

Saladino chose appointments with an eye for historical compatibility: A nineteenth-century black-marble washstand in the shape of a column is accommodated by a carved stone ram's-head spigot with brass wall-mounted taps. A freestanding towel rack and silk-cushioned stool complete the furnishings. Underfoot, the floor treatment is coral.

(Left) A nineteenth-century washstand, its matching black-marble cover casually leaning up against the corner, and steel towel rack complete the vignette.

(Right) Silk-cushioned stool sits under painted scenes. Custom-designed radiator enclosure is covered in oxidized copper leaf. Theatrical scrim is casually draped over rod to expose park view.

Mirrored doors flanking the bath niche conceal w.c., bidet, and stall shower. Oversized cornice clarifies architecture against a background of gold tea paper. Plaster cast busts add note of classical antiquity. "Tobacco Leaf" cotton fabric on love seat from Rose Cumming.

D E S I G N E R
ANGELO DONGHIA

Existing vaults and arches lend sustained architectural integrity to this bathroom designed by Angelo Donghia. Its appeal, however, is derived from a palette of mixed decorative gestures—one which successfully fuses the casual and the classic with inimitable style and even humor.

Mirrored doors flanking the central niche symmetrically organize the room's amenities on either side of the tub: w.c. and bidet on one side, shower stall on the other. A pair of wall-mounted busts preside over each doorway in keystone fashion.

A wall and ceiling treatment of gold tea paper stops at the edge of the tiled dado that runs around the perimeter of the entire space. The sea-foam green ceramic tile was another of the room's existing assets. A period-style vanity with marble top and figured steel legs is surmounted by an inlaid mother-of-pearl mirror. Task lighting is provided by a pair of swing-arm lamps with pleated shades on either side of the mirror.

A small love seat covered in cotton fabric invites relaxing moments, while straw baskets store other bath essentials. Clamshell light fixture over tub enlivens with a subtle Poseidonlike reference.

Jaime Ardiles-Arce

S   T   Y   L   E   S

INDUSTRIAL TECH

I t can be said for any of the arts that what was once avant-garde is, sooner or later, destined to become the establishment. Consider the disciplines of music, art, fashion, and, of course, interior design. Last year's outrageous is this year's obsolete dinosaur.

Amid the pluralistic trends currently awash in interior design, there is one school that, through design, seeks to integrate the service functions of a house with its ceremonial aspects. It expresses this through a kind of flaunting of pipes, vents, conduits, electrical wires, and forced air ducts—all of which increase our awareness of the workings of a house.

The general *ad hoc* appreciation of utilitarian equipment and materials is the cornerstone of what can be called "industrial style." More commonly referred to as "high tech"—a play on the words high style and technology—it embraces functional objects with a new appreciation. While the term has been used in architectural circles to describe buildings incorporating prefabricated or off-the-rack building components, the term also points to a

parallel trend in interior design: the use of utilitarian industrial equipment and materials as home furnishings.

Certainly, high tech has its roots in industrialization and prefabrication—beginning with the Crystal Palace in 1851. Designed and built by Sir Joseph Paxton, an engineer and gardener, as a hall for the Great Exhibition in London, the building made innovative use of prefabricated pieces of precut cast iron, wrought iron, and glass in a rapid assembly system. The structure also marked the birth of an exposed-structure aesthetic that was to become associated with bridges, train sheds, exhibition halls, and oil refineries. A series of exhibitions—Dresden in 1906, Paris in 1925, New York in 1928, and others in between—helped foster a new taste for equipment and machine-made products.

The Eiffel Tower, built in 1889 for the Centennial Exposition in Paris, is the embodiment of the industrial aesthetic. Built of precut wrought-iron trusses supported on masonry piers, the 984-foot tower was as much an aesthetic statement as it was a demonstration of the possibilities of prefabrication: It was completed in a few months, at a modest cost, and with a small labor force.

The aesthetic, however, was officially canonized in 1934 when the Museum of Modern Art (MOMA) staged a Machine Art Show and founded its influential design collection—a shrine to the appreciation of product design.

While architecture today has become more pluralistic, the industrial aesthetic still manages to shine in such structures as the Centre Georges Pompidou in Paris and, to a lesser extent, in the interior of Helmut Jahn's State of Illinois Center.

As the movement gathered more professional legitimacy, selected residential projects assumed a similar expressiveness. The Maison de Verre—designed in 1928 by Pierre Chareau with Pierre Bijoet and completed in 1932—was probably the first major residential demonstration of the industrial aesthetic. The house features mechanistic furnishings such as remote-controlled steel louvers, adjustable mirrors, retractable steel shop ladders, revolving closets, and metal bookcases.

In 1949, designers Charles and Ray Eames created a stir with their landmark Santa Monica home-*cum*-studio. Using industrial parts commonly used to build factories, the house incorporated exposed open webbed-steel joints, prefabricated steel decking, and factory-style windows, most of it ordered from catalogs. While the movement did not catch on for some time, what Pierre Chareau, Charles and Ray Eames and even MOMA did was to create a climate for experimentation: The reutilization of industrial artifacts made to operate in a different context while retaining original function and intent.

This Doctrine of Commercial Reutilization shows up in very real elements in "high tech" bathrooms—commercial ceiling diffusers, exposed pipes for heat, hot and cold water, and ventilation all add visual excitement and can often become the focal point of the design. In terms of fittings, fixtures, and accessories, the look translates into surgeons' scrub sinks, stain-proof lab sinks, or even hospital and airline lavatory fittings, including gooseneck spouts and winged lever controls. Extralarge hospital tubs, wall-mounted urinals, hospital grab bars, pipe towel rails, and liquid soap dispensers are used. Hospital-cubicle ceiling track or industrial metal pipes as shower curtain rods, and sailcloth or canvas curtains fastened with industrial grommets are common. Light fixtures can be the commercial or outdoor variety.

Elliot Fine

D E S I G N E R
ANDREE PUTMAN

Designing in her signature palette of black, white, and chrome, Andree Putman enlivens art deco with the cutting edge of French high tech. Concentrating on the essentials, this bathroom is a commanding understatement of color and materials.

While ceramic tile has become predictable in most bathrooms, Putman's originality combines checkerboard, solid, and diamond patterns for surface interest with a characteristic touch of the unexpected.

A centrally placed tub with sloping back extends the shower alcove, permitting easy access between the two conveniences. "His" and "hers" brushed-steel washbasins—set atop extra-tall legs—flank the bath and are served by wall-mounted fittings with gooseneck spouts and winged lever controls.

Arched mirrors with beveled edges and integrated light sconces facilitate grooming. Chrome-mounted glass shelves beneath each mirror provide convenient storage and display space.

Black-and-white Italian ceramic tile is used in combination of checkerboard, solid, and diamond patterns. Two stainless washbasins on extra-tall legs flank the central tub and shower alcove. Arched grooming mirrors over the basins feature integrated light sconces. Italian ceramic tile, Cedit.

Peter Paige

D E S I G N E R S
BELCIC & JACOBS

Designed by Victor Belcic and Robert Jacobs, this bathroom features a wide-open plan with colors and materials ranging from "factory" to "precious." Surface treatments have all been orchestrated according to the function of each compatible interior zone: gray carpeting near the dressing table, red ceramic tile in the w.c., and black marble tile in the bathing area.

The partitioned convenience, at the right, features a red-tile dado around the sustaining walls and contains the w.c., bidet, and urinal. Immediately outside is the red lacquer and marble-topped dressing table. White walls and mirror relieve the feeling of enclosure in this narrow space.

The dressing corridor leads to a slightly raised, open room in the back of the space. Completely paved in black marble tile, this room contains the washbasin, vanity, whirlpool tub, and stall shower.

A red lacquer and black marble dressing table stands in the corridor linking the w.c. with the bathing and grooming zone in back. Commercial elements include the white porcelain urinal and chrome-plated electric hand dryer on the far back wall beside the closet. Chair, Kartell; tile, Hastings; urinal, American Standard.

Cut wrought-iron structural trusses, sliding glass patio doors, and commercial Vaporlight light fixture clearly embrace an industrial design attitude. Three tiled steps lead to an open shower trough and allow access to the whirlpool. The clerestoried window wall looks out to an enclosed greenhouse terrace.
Whirlpool, fittings, Kohler; tile, Mid-State.

DESIGNER
KEVIN WALZ

For this renovated New York bathroom, designer Kevin Walz simply enhanced the room's natural assets—hexagonal tiled floor, tiled walls, pedestal washbasin, and commodious tub—with a minimum of prefabricated institutional products.

A curved hospital track replaced the original shower-curtain rod over the tub. Large "S" clips hold the white sailcloth curtain through a series of circular steel grommets. A center-set hospital faucet with gooseneck spout and integrated water controls replaced the original period set.

A white plastic-laminate convenience shelf runs the whole length of the room about twelve inches above the w.c. Mirror panels cover the wall from the top of the shelf to the ceiling.

The trapezelike light fixture over the washbasin features a matte-black ceiling mount with lamps suspended from industrial wire cables.

DESIGNER
ALAN BUCHSBAUM

Architect Alan Buchsbaum fully embraces the "inside-out look" by flaunting sliding patio doors and exposed structural trusses on the interior of this loft bathroom. For added surface interest, Buchsbaum mixed his tile formats using two-inch-square white tile on the floor and steps leading up to the open shower trough and four-inch-square tile around the whirlpool and along the walls. The bright red window frame and clerestory seem factory-inspired against this all-white background.

Buchsbaum planned his forms and scale to alter our perception of the room's dimensions: The three steps leading up to the shower, the partially tiled wall treatment, and even the slightly raised tub enclosure create an illusion of greater height.

Tubular steel towel rails and grab bars as well as the commercial outdoor light fixture also make a functional statement of industrial sensibility.

Mark Ross

Hospital ceiling track, gooseneck faucet set, and industrial light fixture coexist with this bathroom's original porcelain fixtures and tile. Plastic-laminate convenience shelf anchors mirror panels over the washbasin and w.c. Faucet, Elkay; ceiling track, Ka-lor Cubicle; light, Harry Gitlin.

(Right) *Frosted-glass screen is all that separates the bathroom from the living area. Towel rail hangs on the edge of the raised floor, leading to the master bedroom. Tub surround, "Corian" by Dupont.*

(Far right) *An integrated planter creates a small access way into this huge sunken tub. Arne Jacobsen designed fittings which share the tub surround with three small Sony monitors and assorted objects. Crescent-shaped windows on four sides afford a great view from anywhere in the loft. Tub fittings, shower head, Kroin; tile, American Olean; television monitors, Sony.*

Robert Levin

D E S I G N E R S
LEMBO/BOHN

Adjoining the raised master bedroom of a Brooklyn, New York, loft, three arched windows set a dramatic stage for this spa-sized bathroom. Design partners Laura Bohn and Joseph Lembo created a huge sunken tub in the center of the space, affording the bather an ideal view through any one of the three crescent-shaped exposures.

The commodious surround is convenient for showing favorite objects, including the three 3.4-inch-square Sony monitors. It also serves as the deck-mounting surface for fittings designed by Arne Jacobsen.

The interior of the tub is covered in one-inch-by one inch ceramic tile in a matte cerulean blue finish. Functional as well as decorative, an integrated planter intrudes into the otherwise square tub, creating a small access area. Tiled steps facilitate entry and exit. Between the tub and structural column, a large plate-glass screen sandblasted in a frosted stripe motif is suspended from three industrial-wire cables.

The designers' industrial sensibility is also apparent in the exposed water and heating pipes, towel rail, black cable-hung floor lamp, and colorful treatment of the structural column.

(Far left) *Four tiled steps lead up to a bathing platform at the far side of the bedroom. The white tiled floor treatment and turquoise ceiling keep the room from becoming too earnest, while the glass-block wall and indoor garden enhance the "greenhouse" effect. Tile, Mid-State.*

(Left) *The custom-designed free-form whirlpool and lush green plants together recall an urban lagoon. Colored gels on the overhead light fixtures add dramatic effect.*

DESIGNER
ALAN BUCHSBAUM

Architect Alan Buchsbaum created this special bedroom/bathroom combination in a downtown New York City loft. The long narrow space features a centrally placed, freestanding closet which separates the sleeping and bathing area from the dressing and grooming area. Colored gels on the ceiling, mounted lights, and a turquoise-painted ceiling mitigate the all-white color palette in the bath area.

The double bed and bathing platform share space on one side of the freestanding closet. The platform is accessed by four steps and completely paved with white ceramic tile. The elevated platform brings the tub up to window level and creates a feeling of protective enclosure for the bed.

The free-form whirlpool was custom-designed by Buchsbaum and—together with its companion plantings—resembles an urban lagoon.

The opposite side of the closet is mirrored and reflects the washbasin, which is set into a cantilevered marble countertop, and the w.c. Task situations are expedited with the horizontal fluorescent light fixture mounted on the mirror panels over the sink. A wall of white lacquered cabinetry stores clothing, towels, and other bath necessities.

(Above) *Exposed ceiling beams lend a more rustic note to the dressing/ grooming area. Mirror panels on the freestanding closet reflect the cantilevered vanity and w.c. An area rug warms the floor, while a collapsible canvas stool holds towels.*

Mirror, tile, and plastic laminate provide color and texture in this loft bathroom. Bath controls and shower attachment for the sunken black whirlpool are wall mounted and backed with a mirror panel. Suspended over the tub is an additional fixed shower head. Tub, Jacuzzi; fittings, Speakman and Rada (thermostatic control); tile, American Olean.

D E S I G N E R S
GILLIS ASSOCIATES

This bathroom designed by Ralph Gillis, AIA clearly demonstrates the industrial high-tech attitude. Exposed pipes, conduits, vents, and forced air ducts all suggest a kind of *ad hoc* appreciation of the workings of the space.

Matte black tile, plastic laminate, and mirror provide the intrinsic sources of color and texture. A black laminate, waist-high sink counter runs along the length of one wall and continues as a simple shelf on the adjoining wall behind the sunken tub. For grooming and hygiene, the counter is fitted with a brushed stainless washbasin and served by a chrome-plated gooseneck spout and single-lever water control.

The sunken whirlpool tub is surrounded by continuous floor-to-ceiling mirror panels on two sides—the back wall providing the mounting surface for the bath fittings and flexible shower head. There is an additional fixed shower head suspended over the tub between a forced air duct and one of the ceiling beams.

Two vertical columns of showcase lamps flank the sink area and are screw-mounted directly into individual sockets in the mirror panel. The tubular black towel rail by the tub doubles as a safety bar.

Mark Ross

S T Y L E S

CONTEMPORARY

New principles and new materials lead to the creation of new stylistic forms. As the industrial and machine age dawned, revivalism was seen as the "enemy," and progressive artists rejected it with the same passion that their parents had embraced it. Contemporary taste represented a feeling for the future. Of all the modern influences, the German Bauhaus movement encouraged historical blindness while it shaped a new twentieth-century sensibility. For the designers of the twenties and thirties, the future was a splendid, perfectly ordered, and clean utopia. White walls, geometric forms, abstract pictures, and functional furniture were the antidotes to the gilded arabesques of a convoluted past.

Contemporary style does not describe a period in the real sense. More a life-style design, it seeks to translate the way we live or should live into objects and design. Since it represents a period in the process of development, it embraces a variety of design influences whose characteristics change constantly in response to fresh inspirations. In its most basic formulation, however, the contemporary sensibility fuses uncorrupted forms with basic, honest materials. Architecturally, the mood translates into clean, unembellished spaces that reflect the linear, planar, and volumetric modes of composition. Pattern and texture are intrinsic rather than applied, in a vocabulary that includes marble, gran-

ite, ceramic tile, polished steel, anodized metal, and lacquer.

Until the time of the Paris Exposition in 1925, almost all American furniture consisted of reproductions of historical periods, with one revival following closely on the heels of another. Meanwhile, the famous Bauhaus of Germany persuasively argued for the virtues of clarity and intelligence. Attempting to reconcile the conflicting aims of art and history, the school mingled fine and applied arts geared to a modern age. Its credo, "Form follows function" became the underlying requirement of all good design. As America was nudged into the movement, the Chicago Exposition of 1933 furthered the tenets of simple design and practical utility.

Good design is first and foremost the expression of an organizing impulse. It has to do with the imposition of a will upon amorphousness. In its most basic formulation, the contemporary sensibility fuses uncorrupted forms with basic, honest materials. Yet changes continue to occur as designers add their interpretations, ranging from the simplification and adaptation of traditional designs to original creations bordering on the bizarre.

Since the contemporary style is constantly changing, definitive characteristics cannot be established. In general, however, lines are clean, simple, and restrained. Strict angularity alternates with graceful curves. The utility of a piece is never obscured and, more often than not, greatly influences design and construction. Incidental details that do not contribute to usefulness or comfort often are reduced, and clean-lined contours, attractive proportions, and subtle dignity remain keynote.

Nevertheless, the contemporary movement remains an outgrowth of the changing social, economic, and technological climate of a given period of time and derives its aesthetic basis from the methods and mores unique to that period. If it is to have a lasting effect, it must epitomize the moment while, at the same time, also incorporate timeless

principles of good taste. All too often, however, contemporary design has been treated as a formal game concerned only with function, economics, and logic. Consequently, it has often been reduced to a spiritless level. Lately, however, a new approach to modernism can be seen—one which covers the bare bones of the German Bauhaus with an overlay of luxury. While remaining loyal to such basic tenets as honest materials, purity of form, and lightness and openness, a whole new set of design icons are reinforcing rather than obscuring the relationship between design and humanity, responding and reacting to basic human expectations.

Freestanding utility core accommodates oversized tub on one side and cantilevered vanity on the other. Tub becomes integral with the wall, its waterline even with the center of the window. Ceiling bares structural bones over gray-carpeted floor treatment.

DESIGNERS
MORPHOSIS

Thom Mayne and Michael Rotondi of Morphosis continually challenge accepted architectural ideas with a signature *ad hoc* approach. For this structural bath addition in Los Angeles, the architects mixed a palette of commonplace industrial materials to create an intriguing, even playful, compositional puzzle.

The two-story bath is Spartan, allowing fixtures to assume unprecedented importance. A low-tiled utility ledge efficiently accommodates a washbasin on one side and a steel-clad tub on the other. White ceramic tile lines the interior of the tub, as well as part of the window wall which forms the tub's integral fourth side. The midsection of a glass-block window through this same wall marks the tub's waterline.

The cantilevered vanity is comprised of a polished granite countertop fitted with a circular washbasin. Oversized bathtub faucets, mounted on the face of the ledge, push all sense of scale to the limit.

Perpendicular steel plates continue up the side of the vanity ledge and are secured by a pair of cable wire fasteners. Each upright plate supports a hinged positional cabinet with a mirrored front panel. Low-pile carpet is the floor treatment throughout.

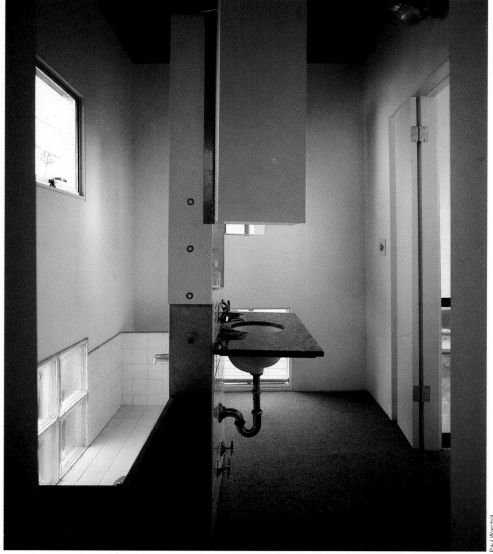

Paul Warchol

ARCHITECTURAL DESIGNER
FREDERICK FISHER

ARTIST
ERIC ORR

Architect Frederick Fisher and artist Eric Orr combined their talents for this bathroom in Los Angeles, California. Their joint venture in aesthetic risk-taking amounts to an empirical exploration of space, light, and the associative resonance of natural and man-made materials.

Slate tile and Mexican Primavera planking constitute the palette of surface treatments in the master bathroom. A sunken tub with an integrally formed backrest is paved in one-inch-square mosaic tile. Period-style brass fittings are deck-mounted along the edge of the tub.

Immediately to the right, an open shower features a drainage trough of river stones covered by a slab of rough slate. Here the fittings are wall-mounted and flanked by a pair of built-in stainless steel storage compartments. An L-shaped bent-steel brace over the shower establishes the outline of an imaginary enclosure.

Waterfalls throughout the space epitomize the preoccupation with transient phenomena. Behind the tub, for example, a tall, narrow incision in the wall is fitted with horizontal grooves over which a wavy film of water dribbles from a hidden pump. Both the waterfall and shower spray are sources of vapor-borne negative ions that are believed to induce relaxation.

Mixed surface treatments
include square slate tile
and custom-milled
Mexican Primavera
planking. Ceiling-mounted
light fixture illuminates
narrow bronze waterfall
panel behind tub. Angled
steel rod visually encloses
the open shower stall.
Shower head, American
Standard; light, Roxter.

Timothy Hursley

DESIGNER
EVA JIRICNA

In this small London bathroom, architect Eva Jiricna mixes cream marble tile with institutionally inspired fixtures in brushed stainless steel. Nautical touches keep the mix from becoming too clinical.

Compatible with the rest of the apartment, the palette embraces materials that are both luxurious and austere. In the bath, for example, stainless steel fixtures undercut the ostentation of the marble wall and floor treatment.

A separate grooming niche features a cantilevered vanity with integral, radius-cornered washbasin. The marble-covered niche backdrops a round "Satellite" mirror designed by Eileen Gray and a rolled-steel light bridge.

A stainless steel hospital tub with porcelain-mounted taps occupies another niche beside the washbasin. Nautical touches here include a false porthole window and a ship's string basket mounted on the wall to hold soap.

A wall of stainless steel storage cabinetry sets off a stainless steel w.c. and institutional drinking fountain. Although the latter item was an afterthought, it ironically has become the room's most provocative modern-day amenity.

Richard Davies

(Opposite page) *Custom-designed stainless vanity features an integrated washbasin with radius corners. Above the vanity is Eileen Gray's famous "Satellite" mirror. Rolled-steel light bridge with single lamp, "Dimensione" by Dil.*

(Far left) *A hospital bath in stainless steel features period fittings with a flexible hand-held shower hose. Nautical touches include the false porthole window and ship's string basket on the wall for holding soap.*

(Left) *A stainless steel drinking fountain is a provocative convenience beside the flush-mounted w.c. Stainless steel cabinetry is for essential storage. Floor and wall treatment throughout is cream marble tile.*

White oak wall treatment and vanity lend color and texture to this small bathroom. Counter extension over the w.c. doubles as a towel-and-display ledge. Light bridge is clad in same white oak and fitted with antidazzling grille. Fittings, swing-arm mirror, Paul Associates; washbasin, Elkay.

Peter Vitale

Cylindrical vanity kiosk features a stainless steel washbasin and hospital fittings. Tiled dado behind the vanity continues as full wall treatment throughout. Diaphanous shower curtain and carpeting soften the palette of cool surfaces.

© Peter Aaron/ESTO

DESIGNERS
PATINO/WOLF ASSOCIATES

A white oak vanity and paneled wall treatment bring material integrity to this bathroom designed by Bob Patino and Vicente Wolf. Serene, poised, and coherent, the space conveys enduring style and practical elegance.

Reiterating the room's quiet tones, white oak wall panels are treated with the precision of a furniture maker. The eight-foot-high panels are butt-joined at four-foot intervals.

A finely crafted white oak vanity features radius corners and narrow reveal beneath the countertop. A continuous extension spans the opening over the w.c., making a convenient towel-and-display ledge. The interplay of textures is further enhanced by the brushed stainless washbasin and polished-chrome fittings.

The entire wall behind the vanity and w.c. is mirrored, while a swing-arm vanity mirror facilitates close-up tasks. A light bridge over the vanity is fitted with an antidazzling grille and covered in the same white oak as the walls. Rheostat-controlled floods provide general illumination.

A custom shower door with sandblasted glass panel lends an inviting translucent effect, while the white marble floor treatment is elegant and maintenance-free. A matching oak w.c. seat cover completes the space with a custom look.

DESIGNER
JOHN SALADINO

Soft colors and a palette of mixed surface treatments enliven designer John Saladino's methodical approach in this small guest bath. So successful is the combination that it invites artistic appreciation amidst a setting of functional glamour.

A cylindrical kiosk fabricated in plastic laminate assumes newfound integrity as a vanity. Abandoning their high-tech image, the stainless steel washbasin and hospital fittings are seen as functionally elegant.

The tile wall treatment beside the tub continues as a dado behind the vanity. A narrow convenience ledge, which doubles for display, breaks the expanse of mirror panels above. Lighting is accomplished over the washbasin with a flush-mounted ceiling fixture fitted with an antidazzling grille, while a recessed floodlight illuminates the bathtub.

Two more unabashedly glamorous touches include the diaphanous silk shower curtain and dusty rose carpeting that pampers the bather's feet.

Washbasin and tub are mounted back-to-back for the feeling of separate yet compatible zoning. Built-in chaise beside the tub permits comfortable tanning beneath the wall-mounted sunlamp. Floor treatment is roughhewn slate throughout. Tile, American Olean.

D E S I G N E R S

GWATHMEY SIEGEL & ASSOCIATES

Charles Gwathmey and Robert Siegel designed this bathroom in line with the austere traditions of the Bauhaus. The built-in chaise, in fact, owes a special debt of gratitude to Le Corbusier's 1929 master bath at the Villa Savoye at Poissy, France.

After demolishing the apartment's existing walls, the central utility core became the cornerstone of the new master bedroom wing. In order to manage compatible zoning in what was to be an open yet private bath, the architects separated the major fixtures on opposite sides of the same wall. The result opens the washbasin to the bedroom, while the tub and chaise are neatly tucked out of sight in the newly created alcove.

The bath's most outstanding feature is the built-in chaise. Located between the tub and the apartment's structural wall, it is pitched to a semireclining position, making it perfect for postbath relaxation or tanning beneath the wall-mounted sunlamp. All of the fixtures, including the chaise, washbasin, and tub are covered in one-inch-square mosaic tile, while the floor treatment consists of twelve-inch-square roughhewn slate tile.

Travertine marble countertop and storage cabinet recall classical stonework. Polished-steel accessories include wall-mounted magnifying mirror and countertop towel rail. Marble appears in bedroom as floor treatment and night tables.

Timothy Hursley

D E S I G N E R
MICHAEL TAYLOR

Recalling the stone artistry of a bygone age, San Francisco-based designer Michael Taylor uses travertine marble for both surfaces and furnishings. Working in his signature beige color palette, Taylor enlivens this suite with a mix of nubby raw silk, mirror, and polished-steel accessories.

An existing structural niche on the window wall provided a natural spot for the washbasin. Treated as a simple monolith, the vanity features a thick marble top over a marble-faced cabinet. Reveals between the drawers preclude the need for any external hardware. A polished nickel-plated washbasin is complemented by a set of acrylic-topped fittings. The entire niche as well as the window reveals are mirrored to amplify the view. Close-up tasks are facilitated by a medicine cabinet with positional mirrors, as well as by the wall-mounted magnifying mirror. Lighting in the space is by way of rheostat-controlled floods for optimum flexibility in controlling ambient and task levels.

The adjoining master bedroom features a nubby raw silk bedspread and pillows. The mirrored back wall visually extends the space to the outdoor sculpture garden. Travertine marble night tables hold delicate paper lanterns and personal mementos.

Travertine marble counter is fitted with nickel-plated washbasin. Medicine cabinet features hinged positional mirrors that open against double-window reveals. Chrome-plated fittings feature acrylic knobs. Enamel clock, Cartier; washbasin fittings, Paul Associates.

A less-than-full-height wall of cabinetry separates the sitting room from the bathroom. Modular seating is arranged with deference to the shelf-mounted media center. Glass-block walls borrow light and ensure privacy. Coffee table is custom-designed by Friedman.

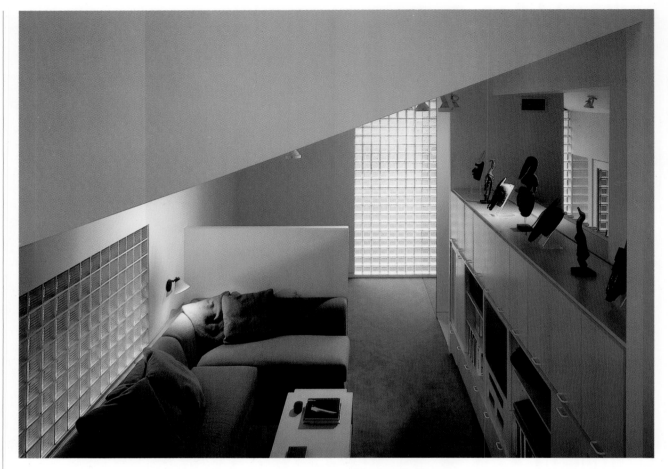

DESIGNERS

STANLEY JAY FRIEDMAN, JOEL C. GEVIS, & ROGER URMSON

Designer Stanley Jay Friedman with associates Joel C. Gevis and Roger Urmson planned this bathroom and sitting room with functional and material compatibility in mind. A shared partitioning wall structurally articulates the separate-but-adjoining spaces with maple cabinetry on one side and a vanity/dressing table on the other.

An existing warren of smaller rooms necessitated a plan of both structural and cosmetic modification. The designers clarified the architecture by removing walls, jags, and coves, and installing glass-block windows to open the space with borrowed light. Newly exposed structural columns became the natural uprights for the less-than-full-height bath/sitting room partition.

Maple cabinetry on the sitting room side accommodates a library, media center, and art-display ledge along the top. On the bath side, the partition features a commodious vanity/dressing table fabricated in the same wood. Fixed mirror panels behind the vanity border the flush-mounted medicine cabinet.

A white whirlpool tub runs parallel to the vanity atop an elevated platform. The adjoining wall is also mirrored, while the floor and platform risers are paved in white ceramic tile. One of a series of Roy Lichtenstein serigraphs presides.

Out of sight behind the tub, a separate water closet contains the w.c., bidet, and shower stall. Ceiling-mounted pinspots illuminate while a strip of showcase lamps along the vanity mirror facilitates task situations.

Showcase lamps provide task lighting. White ceramic floor treatment continues up risers to whirlpool tub. Serigraph, Roy Lichtenstein; whirlpool tub, WaterJet; tile, American Olean; washbasin, fittings, Kohler.

Peter Vitale

(Far right) *Hand-held shower and fixed riser pipe are mounted on trapezoidal-shaped utility ledge. Fast Fill Double Control Valve, designed by Arne Jacobsen, is vertically mounted on the face of the same ledge. Steel-framed glass door at left leads to separate w.c. Bath fittings, Kroin.*

(Right) *A columnar, skeletal wall facade dramatically scans two-story space outside master bath. Shower, utility ledge, and glass-block window can be glimpsed through one of the voids.*

© Peter Aaron/ESTO

DESIGNERS
MORPHOSIS

Thom Mayne and Michael Rotondi of Morphosis show considerable style in the design of this Los Angeles master bath. As seasoned strategists, they have demonstrated the compelling results of using imaginative architectural gestures to reposition the outlook of domestic bath design.

A large open shower and pool-like sunken tub are architecturally celebrated against a backdrop of glass block. The window's gridded motif lends translucent clarity and is once again repeated in the mixed-tile surface treatment on both the walls and floor.

A freestanding trapezoidal-shaped utility core bisects the access steps to the tub and features a top-mounted shower and riser pipe with flexible hose option. The bath controls and shower diverter are vertically mounted on the face of the ledge, which is covered in white ceramic tile. The tub surround, access steps, and floor behind the shower are all tiled in slate.

The rest of the room's amenities are out of sight, yet easily accessible. A steel-framed door with sandblasted glass panels conceals a separate w.c. while another doorway leads to a dressing room. Recessed floods provide lighting throughout.

Timothy Hursley

D E S I G N E R S
ARTHUR ERICKSON ARCHITECTS

(Left) *Stone-clad corridor leading to the master bathroom displays outstanding twentieth-century art collection. Shimmering lacquer pocket doors shut the master suite off from the rest of the house for privacy or entertaining.*

(Far left) *Freestanding display étagère casually separates vanity from sunken whirlpool tub. Oversized porthole mirrors are edge-lit by theatrical makeup lights encased in opaque-glass collars. Shelves display African artifacts, while the skylight provides a perfect view from the whirlpool tub below.*

Designed by architect/partner Francisco Kripacz, this master bathroom resembles a personal art gallery. A program of unpretentious architecture dispensed with the usual tile-and-marble imagery in favor of a space more compatible for the display of the owner's twentieth-century art masterpieces.

A newly enlarged skylight considerably expands the space, while allowing a picture-perfect view from the whirlpool tub below. A freestanding étagère casually separates the bathing area from the rest of the space. The unit's midsection holds a double-faced circular mirror, edge-lit by a strip of theatrical lamps. An opaque-glass collar encases the lights for diffused illumination. Flanking the mirror, vertical uprights display a collection of African artifacts on adjustable glass shelves.

A cantilevered black granite vanity shelf with radius corners sits perpendicular to the étagère. Fitted with an oval washbasin and hospital taps, it is surmounted by a companion mirror matching the one in the étagère. A nearby laminate storage chest doubles as a dressing table, while double-mirror doors conceal a separate shower room replete with w.c. and bidet. The concrete floor treatment was innovatively poured in place between a grid of brushed-steel strips, buffed, and then sealed.

(Right) *Glass-block wall between master bedroom and bath permits shared light between the rooms while ensuring privacy. Channeled bedspread is upholstered in claret silk. Hansen swing-arm lamps illuminate.*

Claudio Santini/Il Bagno oggi e domani

(Above) *Double-door vanity incorporates built-in clothes bin and pullout storage system. Triptych medicine cabinet features hinged positional mirrors for grooming. Étagère with adjustable glass shelves enhances the partition reveal with collectibles.*

(Far right) *Dressing table and w.c. flank corner shower kiosk from Hastings Tile & Il Bagno Collection. Unit features built-in towel rails, shelf storage, basin trough, and Plexiglas enclosure. Floor treatment is pink ceramic tile throughout. W.c., American Standard.*

D E S I G N E R

RUBÉN DE SAAVEDRA

For this master bath/dressing room/bedroom, designer Rubén de Saavedra reconciles the intellectual demands of modernism with the more emotional aspects of contemporary living. Borrowing from a variety of design vocabularies, de Saavedra manages the mix with enticing flair and drama.

A program of structural modifications was spearheaded by the installation of a glass-block wall between the bath and bedroom. The device is both decorative and functional, sharing light from the bedroom window while ensuring privacy in both spaces.

A custom-designed laminate dressing table with cantilevered top addresses personal grooming and storage needs. Shallow makeup trays are augmented by deep-drawer storage for convenience. Mirror panels behind the table create a feeling of greater spaciousness, while recessed floods illuminate.

A Plexiglas shower kiosk occupies the corner between the dressing table and w.c. Its clear, unobtrusive countenance makes a convincing architectural statement without dominating the space. The unit features built-in towel rails and utility storage.

A mirrored partition encloses the vanity and washbasin in a separate niche. Fabricated in rose-colored laminate, the double-door unit incorporates a built-in clothes hamper and pullout storage trays. A triptych medicine cabinet over the vanity features hinged positional mirror panels for full-view grooming. The ten-inch partition reveal features a built-in étagère with adjustable display shelves. Floor treatment throughout is pink ceramic tile.

Jaimie Ardiles Arce

DESIGNERS
BRAY-SCHAIBLE DESIGN

This master bathroom designed by Robert Bray and Michael Schaible reconciles the antithetical notions of luxury and austerity with remarkable ease. A palette of colliding textures and materials including stone, mirror, stainless steel, and even wicker manage the look with compelling results.

Truncated mirror partitions define the vanity and bath area around the window wall. An angled crease between two of the panels creates a niche for the Kasota stone vanity shelf. A brushed stainless steel washbasin with hospital fittings is positioned at the far end, allowing the rest of the vanity to double as a dressing table. A cushioned wicker armchair complements.

The same Kasota stone wall and floor treatment was also used for the custom-carved tub. Raised to windowsill height, the tub now enjoys a panoramic view of the park. Hospital-style fittings for the tub, as well as the round, black speaker grille, and the light fixture are reflected in the mirror panel.

Kasota stone vanity shelf is cantilevered along angled mirror partitions defining the master bedroom. Custom-carved in the same stone, the tub is elevated to enjoy the spectacular view. Cushioned wicker armchair is dressing table essential. Washbasin, Just Sinks; washbasin fittings, Speakman; tub fittings, custom; wicker chair, Bielecky.

(Right) *Subtle angles grace the profile of the simple vanity monolith. Custom-designed shower door features leaded glass panes arranged in a unique pattern. Red-neon circle illuminates deep-set skylight. Floor treatment is poured-in-place terrazzo throughout. Washbasin, fittings, Kroin.*

(Far right) *Mirror panels beside the bathroom create the illusion of a continuous corridor. Vertical water pipe structurally anchors the sculpted vanity. Custom-designed chaise faces wall-mounted audio/video unit by Audio Design Associates. Slatted radiator enclosure doubles as convenience and display ledge.*

Jaime Ardiles Arce

D E S I G N E R S
BROMLEY/ JACOBSEN

This bathroom, designed by Scott Bromley and Robin Jacobsen, rigorously challenges the concept of domestic bath design. Seeking to clarify the rapport between spatial volume and structural harmony, the open-plan bath ambiguously yet artistically acknowledges the user's needs without succumbing to a palette of anonymous design clichés.

Located in a New York City mansion, the bath is situated at the end of a private corridor. Since public access was not a problem, the designers redefined the privacy issue by eliminating the door and facing wall.

Bath essentials are clearly treated with both functional and artistic integrity. Resembling a block of sculpted stone, the vanity assumes newfound grace with its obliquely angled profile. An unrimmed washbasin and single-control fitting complement, while an existing riser pipe remains a structural idiom.

A stall shower is fitted with a custom door featuring a unique design of leaded glass panes. Silvered fiberglass paint and blue-gelled interior light cast a metallic glow from within.

Floor treatment throughout the space is poured-in-place terrazzo, articulated by a grid pattern of narrow metal bands. A recessed flood illuminates, while a circular red-neon tube casts an ambient glow from within the deep-set skylight.

Peter Vitale

Adam Bartos

D E S I G N E R
JOHN SALADINO

Enduring materials strike a classical yet timely note in this bathroom designed by John Saladino. For all its intrinsic restriant, the hand-finished white oak vanity makes a rather commanding statement against a surface treatment of cool ceramic tile.

Saladino's design program sought to emphasize spaciousness as well as elegance. To this end, sheets of tempered glass were used to incorporate the once-blind shower into the visual mainstream. Surface compatibility is ensured with a continuous treatment of tile on the walls, floor, and into the shower itself. As a safety measure, a tubular towel rail in the shower doubles as a grab bar.

A simple white oak vanity between the shower and w.c. accommodates both flat and bulk storage. Figured reveals between the doors and drawers preclude the need for surface-mounted hardware. An unrimmed oval washbasin and fittings complement.

Over the vanity, a medicine cabinet with mirrored positional doors stops short of the edge of the white oak backsplash. Ceiling-mounted light fixture with antidazzling grille continues into the shower area.

Simple lavatory pedestal with back-to-back brass fittings clarifies the angle of the L-shaped tub. Integral color plaster walls around tub are sealed with a coat of shellac. Ear-shaped brass handle is amusing safety feature. Washbasin, fittings, Smolka; tile, American Olean.

D E S I G N E R
STEPHEN HOLL

Dispensing with the usual "washbasin, mirror, and standard tub" approach, architect Stephen Holl offers his own idiosyncratic rendition of domestic bath design. Meticulous detail, vibrant color, and rich materials lend unexpected decorative spirit to this architectural microcosm.

Treating the space as a kind of volumetric canvas, Holl applied color and texture with the care of an artist. Integral-color plaster, for example, adds greater dimension to the walls and ceiling while marble, tile, brass, and porcelain each contribute surface interest. Treating the walls immediately surrounding the tub with a coat of shellac makes them impervious to water stains. The L-shaped tub was designed to complement the entire apartment's angled layout. It wraps around the washbasin creating a reflecting pool.

The simple lavatory pedestal clarifies the tub's right angle as brass fittings are arranged back-to-back fashion with hospital faucets for the washbasin on one side and bath spout on the other. The interior of the tub is paved in mosaic tile, while the surround, enclosure, and lavatory pedestal are covered in verde antique marble. Triangular wall sconce and unusual ear-shaped grab bar with integral towel rail were both designed by Holl.

Sheets of tempered glass across the shower help expand the space. Wall-mounted bench and interior towel rail provide convenience and safety. White oak vanity accommodates both flat and bulk storage. Washbasin fittings, Kroin; tile, American Olean.

Peter Vitale

(Above) *Custom armoires create an architectural,* lit *niche in the master bedroom. Canopylike ceiling cove is edge-lit and silver-leafed for heightened drama. Bed frame and carpeting are also clarified with out-of-sight edge lights.*

(Right) *Dressing area features pearlized lacquer cabinetry and floor-to-ceiling mirror closets for wardrobe storage. Theatrical light strip facilitates grooming. Washbasin, Sherle Wagner; fittings, Paul Associates; stool, Dakota Jackson; w.c., American Standard.*

D E S I G N E R
ERIC BERNARD

Designer Eric Bernard's approach to period design is referential rather than purist. With a recognized proclivity for things Art Deco, the designer has managed to capture the essence of that period without line-for-line reproduction.

For this large master bedroom/bath, Bernard orchestrates a rich palette of materials, surfaces, and even accessories, all in shades of gray. The bathroom consists of a dressing room replete with vanity, floor-to-ceiling closets, and a separate water closet. At center stage of the anteroom is a pearlized gray vanity, fitted with a wide-fascia countertop and full-height doors. A six-sided porcelain washbasin is accommodated by an updated version of standard-issue hospital fittings. Hydraulic "Saturn" stool allows the vanity to double as a dressing table.

A mirrored medicine cabinet over the vanity is surmounted by a theatrical light strip to facilitate grooming, while recessed floods provide general illumination.

Floor-to-ceiling mirrored closets reflect the separate water closet replete with w.c., bidet, and shower. Gray ceramic tile is the surface treatment here, while complementary medium-gray carpeting covers the dressing room and bedroom.

Peter Vitale

Jaime Ardiles-Arce

D E S I G N E R S

BROMLEY/ JACOBSEN

Having acknowledged the structural and functional cornerstones of architecture, Scott Bromley and Robin Jacobsen demonstrate considerable decorative expertise as well. Textures, materials, and a sophisticated lighting program innervate this small powder room with considerable sensory effect.

A brushed-steel vanity shelf with overscaled bull-nose edge spans the length of the entire room. An integral washbasin maintains the unit's architectural integrity as does the faucet designed by Arne Jacobsen.

Lighting played a considerable part in the design effort. Sensor mats underneath the carpeting automatically illuminate the microprocessor-controlled pinspots to preset ambient and task levels. The light level increases as one approaches the washbasin and dims once again by the w.c. Additional ambient light is provided by a track fixture hidden in the curve of the vanity.

Floor-to-ceiling smoked-mirror panels enhance spaciousness without an accompanying glare.

Brushed-steel vanity shelf features overscaled bull-nose edge and integral washbasin. Sensor mats under the carpeting automatically illuminate the space to preset ambient and task levels. Smoked-mirror panels lend mood without glare. Washbasin fittings, Kroin; carpeting, Rosecore; w.c., Kohler; lighting controls, Architel; light fixtures, LSI.

STANLEY JAY FRIEDMAN, JOEL C. GEVIS, & ROGER URMSON

A black-and-white color palette sustains a heightened sense of contrast and architectural integrity in this master bathroom designed by Stanley Jay Friedman and associates Joel C. Gevis and Roger Urmson. With intelligent space-planning as their program's cornerstone, the designers have managed an eloquent statement in the contemporary idiom.

The commodious space was architecturally rezoned into two functionally compatible yet private areas—one with bath, the other with shower, exercise area, w.c., bidet, and vanity. Designed as back-to-back mirror images, the bath essentials form a structural core around which the user can circulate with total ease and efficiency.

The larger of the two areas features an elevated glass-enclosed shower. A stepped partition defines the shower's access route and small exercise area with cushioned rubber-floor treatment. Vanity, w.c., and bidet are all arranged along the wall opposite the same partition.

A platform-mounted whirlpool tub occupies the small bath area. A full-wall mirror treatment gives the illusion of greater depth while a series of ribbed-glass panels borrows light from the client's adjoining art studio. The juncture of the room's two main areas is a symmetrical elevation consisting of a mirrored closet flanked by matching pedestals for television and storage.

The mixed-lighting plan orchestrates recessed floods over the whirlpool with skylight-mounted pinspots by the shower and vanity. Polished black Andes granite is the floor treatment throughout.

(Far Left) *Stepped partition architecturally conceals exercise area next to shower. Multifunctional pedestal accommodates television monitor, towel rail, and open-shelf storage. Pinspots are mounted along the obliquely angled skylight walls. Shower fittings, Kohler; lights, Harry Gitlin.*

(Left) *Elevated whirlpool tub sits atop platform of black Andes granite. Ribbed-glass panels share light with the client's adjoining art studio. Lacquered television pedestal features rotating tray for convenient viewing. Whirlpool tub, WaterJet; fittings, Kohler.*

Peter Vitale

(Left) *Grooming niche in dressing room is mirrored on three sides for 360-degree view. Custom stainless steel washbasin designed by Rybar is set into sealed and hand-finished wood counter. Fittings, P.E. Guerin.*

(Far left) *Oversized stainless steel tub is flanked by display étagères hung with leather masks by Nancy Grossman. Mirror panels go up behind the tub, over the ceiling, and down behind the freestanding vanity. Three-dimensional brown vinyl covers walls and ceiling.*

DESIGNER
VALERIAN RYBAR

Valerian Rybar designed his own bath/dressing room in a most luxurious manner. With organization being his highest consideration, Mr. Rybar hid a complex of storage closets and grooming aids behind mirror panel doors leaving only the stainless steel tub, vanity, and cushioned banquette in full view.

A freestanding vanity and mirrored partition are all that separate the bathroom from the dressing room. The boat-shaped vanity features an exotic wood top and sides, sandwiched between two curving slabs of brushed steel. An unrimmed oval washbasin is enhanced by gilt bronze fittings. The mirrored partition behind the vanity architecturally clarifies the double entry into the stepped down dressing room.

A stainless steel tub with extra deep boat-shaped depression is the vanity's only companion appointment. Custom designed by Mr. Rybar, it features a welded deck set atop a flush panel surround. Flank-

ing the tub, a pair of étagères display worked leather masks by Nancy Grossman. Surface applications throughout this area combine mirror, polished steel and a three dimensional vinyl wallcovering in a tortoise shell motif.

Flush mirror panel doors beside the tub conceal additional bath essentials. One door opens to reveal a marble- and mirror-covered shower room with w.c., bidet, and shower. Immediately beside this space another door hides a wall-mounted urinal.

The dressing room features a central banquette covered in hand-painted pony skin. The banquette is hydraulically adjustable to massage-table height and frequently doubles as a luggage rack and ironing board. There is a full-wall closet in the dressing room in addition to an inventive belt-and-tie cabinet on the back of the vanity partition. A personal grooming niche fitted with a built-in tortoise counter and stainless washbasin is another unique amenity.

Recessed floods provide general illumination in the bathroom while the dressing room utilizes both floods and wall washes. Custom-colored carpeting is the floor treatment throughout both spaces.

(Top right) *Freestanding vanity and mirrored partition create a double entry into the stepped-down dressing room. Cushioned banquette covered with hand-painted pony skin can be glimpsed beyond the vanity. Washbasin fittings, P.E. Guerin.*

(Far right) *Beside the tub, separate mirror panels open to reveal a shower room, replete with w.c., bidet, and urinal closet. W.c., bidet, and shower fittings, American Standard; tub fittings, P.E. Guerin.*

(Bottom right) *Dressing room side of vanity partition features an inventive tie-and-belt storage cabinet. Entrance to the bathroom, stepped up to accommodate the tub, is on either side of the tie cabinet. Edge of banquette can be glimpsed in the foreground.*

S T Y L E S

JAPANESE

The Japanese approach to design is essentially one of elegant restraint. Certain key items are carefully chosen and even celebrated for their own virtuoso significance. Yet, for all its refinement, Japanese interior design retains an organic character that is clearly an indigenous product of native life and conditions. In the traditional Japanese house, for example, one room has several functions. Sliding doors and a variety of portable partitions alter the size and shape of a room, while the redistribution of its furniture determines its function. As a result, there is a pragmatic interrelationship among the floor, the partitioning devices, and the furniture. Architecturally, the traditional Japanese house is gauged in human measurements and derives any of its aesthetic virtues from the modularity of its plan. The tatami mat, originally designed to accommodate one sleeping person or two standing people, is used to conceptualize room size. Houses are planned as a cluster of rooms, each of which is sized to accommodate a specific number of tatami mats, each mat being identical in size and shape. It is just such repetition, similarity, and compositional rapport that persuasively illuminates the role of orderliness in aesthetic success.

Japanese interiors traditionally exude a sense of serenity, poise, and coherence. Quiet tones and natural materials imbue austerely elegant spaces with dignity and tranquility. The Oriental reverence for material and disdain for applied color is key.

Highly figured woods are finely finished but unvarnished to let the pattern of the grain show through. The cold grayness of stone and concrete reaffirm the natural design vocabulary, while the translucence of paper supplies both color and texture. Rooms have fewer things in them, giving the few items there greater visual significance. The look is restrained, lean, and primeval.

The Japanese bath (*furo*) is designed to be used by more than one person at a time. The area used for washing one's body is outside the tub and usually has a shower attachment high up on the wall, with hot and cold water taps lower down. To wash oneself, one takes water from the bathtub in a small pail. After scrubbing and rinsing outside, the tub is entered for warming and relaxing the body.

The tub is generally deep enough to cover the shoulders of a seated person so that if one sits with the knees tucked up, two or more people may sit together. The length of a comfortable tub should be approximately four feet, with the width fixed at between thirty-two and thirty-six inches. The tubs are either recessed into the floor or accessed by a ledge or platform.

Wood, especially the fragrant Japanese cypress, is the best material for a tub. Wood may also be used for the hand bucket, stool, and slatted platform in the washing area. Natural materials such as rock or stone may also be used to aesthetically reinforce the atmosphere of a natural hot spring.

A slightly raised ledge along the back wall is convenient for sitting or placing towels within easy reach. Sliding glass doors have been fitted with panels of mullioned rice paper to simulate the traditional shoji screen.

© Ezra Stoller/ESTO

The oval whirlpool tub is elevated in a tiled platform to capitalize on the terrace view. A black matchstick shade diffuses light through the black-framed window. Plants, towels, and a collection of cobalt blue glass are arranged along the tiled ledge. Whirlpool tub, fittings, American Standard.

DESIGNER
PAUL LEONARD

Rather than employing only a palette of traditional Japanese motifs, designer Paul Leonard evokes the Japanese aesthetic by carefully melding color and texture with selected accessories.

Using an all-gray color palette, Leonard maintains spatial integrity and visual interest using ceramic tile with a special sleight-of-hand—a gray-and-white swirl pattern for the walls and a subtly mottled pattern on the floor, tub enclosure, and low partitions that simulates natural materials.

Since privacy was not an issue, Leonard placed the whirlpool tub directly beneath the window, affording a perfect view of the planted terrace. A pedestal washbasin with a floor-to-ceiling mirrored backsplash sits directly across from the tub and can be enjoyed for its sculptural quality. Two low-tiled partitions—one beside the sink and the other at the head of the tub—architecturally conceal the bidet and w.c.

A full-length black lacquer cheval mirror, peach silk cushions, cobalt glass, and lacquer complete the accessory appointments.

Lighting by David Winfield Willson, IALD includes a series of track-mounted brass fixtures, all rheostat-controlled for additional ambience.

A floor-to-ceiling mirror panel behind the washbasin expands the space and serves as a decorative backsplash. A brass floor lamp illuminates a black lacquer storage chest and handmade basket. The low-tiled partition conceals the w.c. Pedestal washbasin, fittings, American Standard.

A continuous mosaic-tiled floor treatment enhances the craterlike appearance of the soaking tub. Abstract patterns in gray, black, and white provide the only color in the room besides the cedar wood trim. Traditional Japanese bathing essentials include the basin, stool, and hand bucket.

D E S I G N E R
GEORGE NAKASHIMA

Furniture craftsman and designer George Nakashima used a purist approach in this Japanese bath: pattern, color, and texture are derived from the materials themselves rather than applied. In this case, natural cedar window frames, trim shoji screens, and a mosaic-tiled floor treatment reveal the material integrity which is the touchstone of the Japanese design aesthetic.

Nakashima set the traditional *furo,* or soaking tub, in the center of the space. With its raised sides and free-form shape, the pool's craterlike appearance (see page 101) is heightened by mosaic tile. Using the small window as a guide, the tile stops at the lower sill on the back wall, while on the adjacent wall it stops at the top of the frame.

Japanese cedar was used throughout for window frames, crown molding, ceiling beams, and even to cover the heating convector. The traditional basin, stool, and hand bucket were crafted by Nakashima.

DESIGNERS
HOCHEISER-ELIAS DESIGN GROUP

Designer Brad Elias of the Hochheiser-Elias Design Group, evokes serenity and poise with simple materials. Narrow-slatted cedar paneling, horizontally applied, is used for its inherent warmth and color.

Elias raised the black fiberglass whirlpool atop a carpeted platform, taking full advantage of the picture-perfect ocean view.

A pair of brass-and-white-enamel wall sconces provides an ambient glow, while hand-wrought baskets, a lacquer tray, and black rose plant complete the disciplined vignette.

While not traditionally Japanese, Elias manages the contradiction readily apparent in Eastern design: spare yet rich, brutal yet delicate.

Architectural symmetry and natural materials evoke serenity in this oceanside bath. The black fiberglass whirlpool is elevated atop a carpeted platform, surrounded by the warmth of slatted cedar paneling. Whirlpool, WaterJet; fittings, Kohler.

F U N C T I O N S

SPORTS BATHS

Working out in the comfort of one's own home has recently become a popular option for more and more of the fitness-minded. Home gymnasiums are springing up wherever fitness paraphernalia can be stashed, forcing us to see old rooms in a completely new light. Even though many people are motivated by the group dynamics of health clubs, several factors have sent people home to shape up: The fitness obsession has made many of the health clubs unbearably overcrowded; novices generally prefer to go through the awkward beginning stages of an exercise program without an audience; buying one's own equipment can prove to be more cost-effective in the long run; and, finally, one is not confined by a club's schedule of hours.

Until about five years ago, few people could afford the luxury of bringing the health club into the home. Most major exercise equipment was designed for commercial use in both price and size. Recently, however, the home market has muscled in on the health club territory with the introduction of body-building equipment whose keynotes are portability, affordability, and good design.

As the bathroom becomes more open to scrutiny, it also is becoming larger and more accessible. No longer considered merely a facility, the bathroom is opening up into both a spacious exercise spa and dressing area. In addition to its most basic functions, the bath must now ameliorate the escalating stresses of everyday life. At the extreme, it has become a monument to our preoccupation with health and beauty.

A realistic expression of this concept is the bathroom equipped with the latest therapeutic as well as exercise amenities. The newly discovered therapeutic value of whirlpools, for example, has focused more attention on the bathtub. While tubs formerly were set aside and concealed behind sliding glass doors, the newest models are equipped with water jet streams and enjoy a new design prominence—either raised, sunken, or centrally located. An alternative is the extra-deep soaking tub or *furo,* which allows the user to luxuriate while completely immersed up to the shoulders. Today's showers are more than likely to feature special hydrotherapeutic massage heads, which offer a variety of water jet sprays to stimulate circulation and revitalize muscles. A whole new market of attractively designed and sensibly scaled exercise equipment has also moved into the bathroom. With spatial limitations the only obstacle, sports baths can embrace everything from a set of dumbbells to a multistation weight-lifting machine. Exercise mats, saunas, and steam baths complete the full scope of available amenities.

Custom-designed whirlpool tub features made-to-measure interior and heavy-gauge rolled-steel lip. Obliquely angled access steps are edge-lit and correspond to the ceiling-mounted tubular grab rings. Whirlpool tub, Aqua Baths; tile, Design Technics; sculpture, Tony Marra.

© Peter Aaron/ESTO

© Peter Aaron/ESTO

DESIGNER
ERIC BERNARD

In demonstrating the compatibility of technology and interior design, the work of designer Eric Bernard remains nonpareil. For this sophisticated project, the designer and his associate Dennis Sangster integrated the most advanced electronics and bathing amenities into a unique bath/exercise/media room.

Bernard divided the space into three functionally distinct yet compatible zones: bathing and hydrotherapy, exercise, and entertainment. Accommodating the first function is an oversized, custom-designed, trapezoidal-shaped whirlpool tub (see page 107). Large enough to accommodate six people, the tub is raised atop a tiled platform with obliquely angled steps. Three ceiling-mounted tubular grab rings ensure safe access.

Leaving nothing to chance, the tub's interior conforms to the client's exact back measurements. Timely hydrotherapy can be accomplished by a direct telephone linkup—a simple telephone call from anywhere fills the tub, heats the water, and activates the water jets.

The middle portion of the space features a multistation home gym and supine bench. Underfoot, each section of the grid-patterned exercise mat coincides with the twelve-inch-by-twelve-inch dimension of the ceramic floor tile.

The same ribbed tile seen throughout the space continues over the surface of the double vanity. In this area, a three-panel medicine cabinet with positional mirrors facilitates grooming while circular cutouts in the side wall hold towels.

A low-tiled partition beside the exercise area defines the compact media area that incorporates a built-in projection television, audio system, and ceiling-mounted speakers.

Francesca Bettridge's lighting program includes fluorescent-incandescent tubes over the vanity, mini-incandescents along the tub's access stairs, and recessed floods for general illumination throughout. There is also a standing dockside fixture more commonly seen in marinas.

Marcy home gymnasium is flanked by whirlpool and media area. Low-tiled partition doubles as display ledge and backrest for cushions. Circular wall cutouts beside the vanity accommodate rolled towels. Home gym, Marcy; washbasins, Aqua Baths; sculpture, Tony Marra; lighting, Cline, Bettridge & Bernstein, Lighting Design, Inc.

A tiled partition anchors the cantilevered vanity shelf on one side and conceals the elevated whirlpool on the other. The terry-cushioned platform doubles as an exercise table and cozy reading nook. Tiled steps between the platform and partition lead up to the whirlpool bath. Ceramic tile, Edilcuoghi.

D E S I G N E R S
DESIGN MULTIPLES

Relaxing, exercising, and grooming are all easily accomplished in this bathroom designed by David Eugene Bell, ASID, and Donald Cotter of Design Multiples. Italian ceramic tile is used as a surface treatment, lending continuity, integrity, and practicality to the exercise-oriented multizoned space.

Architectural planes and partitions are effectively used to suggest functional compatibility. A cantilevered vanity shelf floats between an existing wall and the new partition hiding the elevated whirlpool bath. The shelf is fitted with a self-rimmed white porcelain washbasin and is backed with floor-to-ceiling mirror panels. A small built-in white lacquered shelving unit holds grooming necessities.

A tiled platform at the base of the bath partition is fitted with a terry-covered cushion. This is used for exercising as well as reading or relaxing. Tiled steps lead up to the private whirlpool area.

Elliot Fine

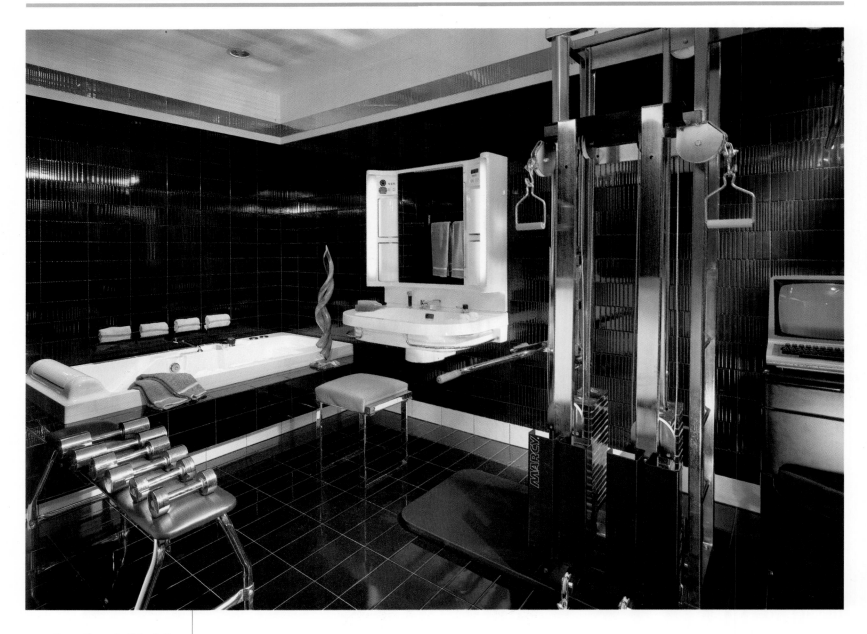

Smooth and ribbed tile surfaces are combined for graphic impact and surface interest. A Marcy multistation home gymnasium and Radio Shack computer accommodate exercise program and business respectively. Bathroom fixtures, wall, and floor tile, Hastings Tile & Il Bagno Collection.

DESIGNER
WILLIAM E. MILLER

William E. Miller, principal of W.E.M. Interior Designs, designed this bathroom—appointed with a home gymnasium and computer—to fulfill a variety of health as well as business and entertainment needs. Using tile for graphic impact and decorative effect, Miller specified the same rectangular format throughout the room, though in different finishes: smooth glossy on the floor; ribbed glossy for the walls; and a ribbed white tile for the ceiling and crown, highlighted with a band of platinum tiles.

All of the fixtures are white. The whirlpool tub features a built-in neck roll and molded interior armrests. Miller set it atop a black-tiled enclosure finished with a tiled baseboard recess.

The wall-mounted vanity unit incorporates a washbasin, swivel-shelf storage, electrical outlet, digital clock, mirror, integrated lamps, and curved steel towel rails.

The multistation gym features chromed weights and vinyl-covered contact surfaces. Its companion supine bench temporarily stores a set of chrome-plated dumbbells. The home computer stands atop a lacquered pedestal that features a built-in stool.

Vanity lighting is supplemented by recessed floods for general illumination throughout.

(Below left) *Detail of the molded vanity unit shows digital clock, electrical outlet, swivel storage compartments, part of the grooming mirror, and the integrated fluorescent tube.*

(Below right) *The Radio Shack home computer is set atop a black lacquered storage pedestal with swing-out storage compartments by Hastings Tile & Il Bagno Collection. The bottom compartment contains a built-in stool.*

FUNCTIONS

DRESSING ROOMS

In the fourteenth century, feudal households were pyramidal in organization as well as architectural plan. The household was a mutually beneficent society that worked not only for the power and glory of the lord but also for the advantage and protection of everyone in the household. The medieval house plan provided a great hall for the daily use of the entire household, which was flanked by private rooms at either end for the use of family and servants. These lodgings—whether a single chamber or a string of rooms—were the private territory of whoever occupied them. Access was allowed only to those who were invited.

By the late sixteenth century and early seventeenth century, greater wealth and the desire for luxury resulted in more complex interiors. By this time, the hall had been usurped as the ceremonial pivot of the house by the great chamber—a more intimate space located off the hall. Great chambers were regularly used as combined bed and sitting rooms, and people even used the same chamber for sleeping, playing games, receiving visitors, and meals. Originally termed "formal house plans," lodgings eventually came to be known as apartments and separate bedrooms began to appear.

The separate dressing room appears to be an English refinement that began during the latter half of the seventeenth century. The grandest houses of the period would sometimes feature two dressing rooms, one each for the husband and wife.

By the eighteenth century, there was a tendency for country homes to have a larger number of small apartments rather than a few very grand ones. Dressing rooms of the period often outstripped the bedroom in size and were invariably used as sitting rooms. Handsomely furnished, the dressing room became the apartment's new meeting place; the owner would come down from his bedroom and receive people on business while his toilet was being finished off by his valet. By the end of the eighteenth century, bedrooms still had dressing rooms attached to them, but they were no longer reception rooms. Instead, the master of the house invited people to his study. This often had a dressing room and sometimes a bathroom next door, but the dressing room was now only for the owner.

The idea of the owner's private dressing room still stands today. Although considered a true luxury, dressing rooms are most commonly encountered as part of the master bedroom/bathroom complex. Usually designed with an eye for organization, these rooms can feature integrated shelving and rack systems for ease of clothing selection and storage. Mirrors, adequate task lighting, comfortable seating, a dressing table, and even laundry bins are sought-after amenities for a dressing room.

A small grooming niche is appointed with treasured and sentimental objects: a pair of silver tea caddies, brass candlesticks, a cloisonné clock, and a set of silver-mounted hairbrushes and hand mirror. On the walls, a collection of noteworthy autographs.

Norman McGrath

Crescent-shape of the dressing table is repeated in the Persian travertine vanity/bathing platform along the mirrored wall. Wall-mounted brass swing-arm mirror facilitates makeup application. Bird's-eye maple chair is design inspired by Jean-Michele Frank. Adjustable mirror, Karl Springer; bath fittings, towel rails, Paul Associates; recessed lighting, Lightolier.

D E S I G N E R
RONALD BRICKE

Ronald Bricke designed this spacious bath/dressing room with period elegance in mind. Paneled in bird's-eye maple, the room conveys the spirit of finely crafted furniture from the Art Deco age.

Structural modifications converted three smaller rooms into this large T-shaped bath/dressing room. The longest portion of the space is reserved for wardrobe storage and features floor-to-ceiling closet panels on both sides of the corridor. All of the doors and curved walls are finished in bird's-eye maple, with the exception of two mirrored doors.

Bath and grooming essentials occupy the entire wall at the end of the dressing corridor. To the left, a sauna and storage cabinet are housed in a separate wall niche. A sculpted Persian travertine bath-and-vanity platform occupies the rest of the wall from the sauna to the windows. The bilevel platform holds a washbasin on its upper portion and a whirl-pool tub on the lower level. Mirror panels along the wall reflect the seaside view as well as the entire dressing area.

Echoing the curved edge of the vanity platform, a bird's-eye maple dressing table designed by Bricke takes center stage. Displaying its Art Deco heritage, the table features two slide-out makeup trays and two storage drawers. Brass-and-ivory hardware is custom-designed.

Ceiling-mounted floods over the tub, washbasin, and dressing area are augmented by polished-steel wall sconces. Bottom-mounted accordian-pleated shades ensure privacy, while rose-colored carpeting is the floor treatment throughout.

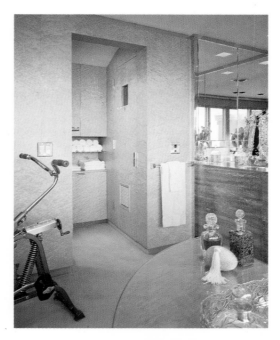

Custom sauna is housed in a separate wall niche beside the marble vanity. Built-in storage unit adjoining sauna incorporates upper double-door cabinet, open ledge with shelf, and integrated clothes hamper below. Towel rail in polished steel and lucite, Paul Associates.

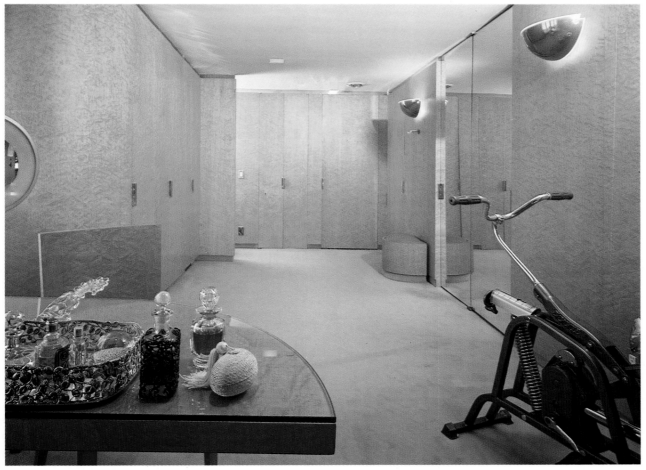

Walls of figured bird's-eye maple conceal voluminous storage behind floor-to-ceiling panels. Polished-steel wall sconces echo shape of half-round custom dressing stool. Rose-colored carpeting enhances Deco ambience. Wall sconces, Atelier International; carpet, Stark.

A second copper washbasin with the same style period brass fittings and marble countertop is located in the larger dressing area. The three-sided alcove is mirrored and illuminated for easy grooming.

DESIGN
SONNENBERG MANSION

Located in the Sonnenberg Mansion alongside New York's historical Gramercy Park, this traditionally styled dressing suite adjoins a large master bedroom and sitting room.

The first space is a grooming corridor replete with washbasin, vanity, and even family photos. The sixteen-drawer mahogany vanity provides voluminous storage space, while the black marble countertop is elegant and maintenance-free. An unrimmed, copper-clad washbasin is served by period fittings in solid brass.

A double-tiered brass chandelier provides ambient light, while task situations are facilitated by the back-lit frosted-glass frame around the wall-mounted vanity mirror.

The large dressing room in back features period mahogany paneling, large walk-in closets, and personal dressing niches: one filled with silver-mounted hairbrushes with matching hand mirror, silver tea caddies, and an autograph collection (see page 115); and another one featuring a second washbasin set into its own mirrored alcove. A floor treatment of deep red carpeting runs throughout the two rooms as a plush accent to the space.

The narrow grooming corridor leads into a more spacious dressing/sitting area. The elegant black marble countertop is complemented by an unrimmed copper-clad washbasin and solid-brass period fittings. Custom mirror over the sink features an illuminated frame with frosted-glass inset panels.

Norman McGrath

Jeff Blechman

(Above) Tromp l'oeil mural covers seven floor-to-ceiling closet panel doors. Marble-topped semainier presides at the back wall in solitary elegance. Lacquered pink walls and matching carpet add glamour and serenity to the space.

D E S I G N E R
JOHN SALADINO

A trompe l'oeil illusion of an ancient view of Bridgehampton prevails in this dressing room designed by John Saladino. Salvaging what may have been a featureless corridor, the painted floor-to-ceiling closet panels successfully open the room to the outdoors with architectural fantasy and humor.

Trompe l'oeil artist David Fisch reproduced ancient Renaissance surfaces in a carved balustrade, double row of columns, tiled floor, and portico. The panoramic view of the distant horizon is embraced by the covered portico, which is itself stepped down from the dressing area with tromp l'oeil sleight of hand.

Furnishings continue the illusory dialogue between inside and outside—the eighteenth-century German refectory table is placed to function in the context of the open loggia as well as in the dressing room itself.

Colors are characteristically pastel. Peachy pink lacquered walls and custom-colored carpeting wrap the room in an ambience both glamorous and serene. Recessed floodlights illuminate, while a built-in lacquered vanity with mirrored niche at one end facilitates storage and grooming.

DESIGNER
VALERIAN RYBAR

Fashioned by interior designer Valerian Rybar, this Paris dressing room is more than just an aristocratic space conforming to traditional stylistic mores. By combining the classical art of scagliola with trompe l'oeil and mirror panels, Mr. Rybar demonstrates his sense of historical continuity in the context of current design.

The vanity and cantilevered dressing table are situated at right angles to one another, separated by a structural column. The adjoining areas both feature commodious mirror-paneled walls and built-in light fixtures equipped with opaque glass diffusers.

Surface treatments are the key to the room's unique sense of luxury. Light and dark *faux* tortoise walls set off matching inlaid scagliola plaques set in trompe l'oeil molding of semi-precious stones. Each panel is superimposed with relief carvings of urn and flower motifs in the Oriental style. As a decorative art medium, scagliola is best explained as a plasterlike paste tinted with pigments, inlaid into other materials, and polished to the brilliancy of stone. The form reached its highest expression in the eighteenth century.

Bronze doré wall sconce and Directoire side chair complement with classical antiquity. The floor treatment throughout is apricot carpet.

Pascal Hinous

Polished blue wall plaques with urn and flower motifs revive the classical art of scagliola. Faux tortoise and malachite walls complete the palette of surface treatments with colorful style. Antique wall sconce provides task light beside the washbasin. Fittings are gilt bronze.

D E S I G N E R

RUBÉN DE SAAVEDRA

Designed by Rubén de Saavedra, this dressing room features an intelligent system of open and closed storage for the ultimate in wardrobe organization. The success of de Saavedra's legerdemain is evident in the system's efficiency and manageability contained in a small space.

The long, narrow space features a single entry access through the adjoining master bath. A large open alcove on the left side of the room accommodates hanging storage from a tubular steel rod. Immediately above, a gridlike system of open shelves holds a sweater collection.

The right side of the room features a ceiling-high shoe cabinet fitted with angled shelves for easy access. Additional closed-door storage, including a pivoting clothes hamper equipped with a removable interior canister, is provided below for easy access.

The entire rear wall of the dressing room is fitted with an integrated system of clear plastic shirt trays, organized according to season and occasion. Between the shoe cabinet and shirt organizer, two pantrylike units slide out to reveal four tie-storage compartments. Diamond cutouts at the top of each unit store rolled belts.

A small table at the center of the room is the key innovation. A kind of Rubick's Cube when closed, the boxlike table actually incorporates extension leaves, concealed footrest, and fully upholstered stool with backrest.

The storage system acts as the perfect functional complement to the spacious and intelligently designed master bath.

The custom-designed cabinetry is all fabricated in plastic laminate and fitted with polished-steel hardware. Recessed floodlights on ceiling are rheostat-controlled for flexible illumination. Ivory carpeting floor treatment continues the neutral palette throughout the dressing room and master bath.

DESIGNER
J. ALLEN MURPHY

At Wychwood, the Long Island home of J. Allen Murphy, the designer successfully straddles the dividing line between period room and stage set. His fascination with historical allusions, period furniture, pictures, and other objects—all lovingly gathered for their associative qualities—has resulted in an imaginative and continental setting.

So thoughtfully has Murphy integrated, and in some cases concealed, the room's practical amenities that it more closely resembles a gracious sitting room than it does combination bath/dressing room.

The longer portion of the space is flanked by identical niches—one for the bathtub, the other for the bed. Finished with hand-carved *boiserie* frames, each intimate alcove features its own discreetly romantic lighting. An artful vignette with covered table, Victorian papier-mâché chair, tiger-clad luggage rack, and Chinese library table completes this side of the room.

A four-panel folding screen separates the lavatory area from the rest of the space. Here a white porcelain washbasin takes center stage and is flanked by two out-of-sight alcoves: one for the w.c. and bidet, the other for a stall shower.

The washbasin is flanked by double windows curtained in paisley. A simple medicine cabinet features integrated light sconces, while a recessed niche below stores easy-to-reach toiletries. A small William and Mary stool and collection of Staffordshire military figures on the windowsills complete the vignette. Washbasin, American Standard.

Phillip Ennis

FUNCTIONS

OUTDOOR BATHS

Since nature is the final frontier of inner space, discovering and exploring it has greatly influenced contemporary interior design. The elements of light, sun, and air have long embodied nature's health-giving virtues; capturing this vitality is one of architecture's new goals. Clerestories, skylights, glass block walls, and even greenhouse additions are some of the devices currently being used to embrace a new visual vocabulary from morning sun to a darkened glimpse of the stars.

The games of architectural content are played with space and light. Natural light endows a space with a series of changing images and animates that space into something other than a static bit of cubage. The new use of apertures takes full advantage of light's natural ability to shape and change. But this approach leaves no room for frills and complex details. A space of unadorned stucco walls and plain wood or stone floors can be infinitely more moving in terms of architectural content than a room full of rich adornments. The most successful spaces of this style are free from extraneous details; they are often all-white spaces that emphasize the interplay of light and shadow.

Formerly the most private room in the house, now even the bathroom is being opened up with bold new apertures. Gone is the single pane of frosted glass. Since rural architectural commissions offer the best opportunities for such expression, one frequently encounters sliding glass doors and ceilings as well as greenhouse additions in suburban settings. At the extreme, larger bathrooms of this type have come to resemble solariums in which the occupants can bathe, relax, read, and sunbathe.

DESIGNER
PETER GLUCK

This spacious bathing area is located in one of two pavilions designed by architect Peter Gluck as additions to an original 1955 Ludwig Mies van der Rohe house. Sharing space with the guest quarters and a sauna facility, both the shower and bathing zones are paved with one-inch-square porcelain ceramic tile. A black-and-white checkerboard motif is applied as a band around the entire space and as the floor treatment in the shower and corridor.

The shower alcove, at left, features a single-control water lever and double shower heads—one fixed, the other, a flexible hand-held model. A curved acrylic screen and integrated corner drain manage water control.

On the right, a sunken Japanese-style tub features a tiled access step that doubles as a seating ledge. Whirlpool jets in the tub as well as a hand-held shower head allow mixed hydrotherapeutic modes. Separate chrome-plated bath and shower controls are mounted low to the tub's recess in order to facilitate operation when seated.

The large-gridded steel screen in the back actually becomes part of the exterior wall of the guest bedroom. It is also a successful ploy that allows the interior to be appreciated as an extension of the site.

A black-and-white checkerboard motif in limited application enlivens this white-tiled shower/bath area. A curved acrylic screen, at left, controls splashing in the shower alcove. Bath controls, at right, are mounted low to facilitate operation when seated. Tile, American Olean; tub, shower fittings, Speakman.

Paul Warchol

A sculpted shower and whirlpool share the view through a huge Palladian-style window. The shower alcove features a recessed water trough and wall-mounted fittings. White ceramic tile covers floor, tub platform, and mantel. Bathtub, Kohler; bath/ shower fittings, Broadway; tile, American Olean.

D E S I G N E R S
WILLIS & ASSOCIATES

Capitalizing on a private wooded setting, designer Beverly Willis created an open bath-and-shower zone in the light of a huge Palladian-style window.

Setting the tub slightly off center created a corner shower stall—the shower head and water controls are mounted on the back wall, with the base of the alcove recessed and fitted with a water drain.

The whirlpool tub is set atop a wide-edged platform; a low-tiled cube beside the tub enclosure conceals towel storage and doubles as a bench for relaxing or drying off. Spread-fit bath controls are deck-mounted on the side of the tub closest to the shower.

The period washbasin is wall-mounted and fitted with decoratively shaped steel leg supports. The grooming mirror above the sink repeats the arched motif of the window and shower backsplash.

A surface treatment of white ceramic tile is used throughout—in a diagonal pattern on the floor, around the mantel, tub, and shower, and as a backsplash behind the sink. The truncated wall sconce over the mirror is a custom design by Willis.

DESIGNER
RIO RAIKES

The "bathhouse" designed by Rio Raikes functions as a personal retreat, art studio, and cabana. Though the structure is barely two years old, Raikes captures the patina of age by juxtaposing weathered building materials with simple, almost primitive architectural gestures.

A small, rectangular structure with a gabled roof, the exterior is clad with weathered cedar planking. Seamless panes of glass overlooking the deck and hot tub are faced with wide mullions in a grid pattern, which double as display ledges. The structure's extended roofline shades the interior during the hottest part of the day and precludes the need for any window treatment.

The somewhat wild landscaping, casually strewn clay pots, and untrimmed shrubbery are in keeping with the unpretentiousness of the structure.

Timothy Hursley

Weathered materials lend the patina of age to this two-year-old bathhouse. Luxurious amenities include the small sun deck and redwood hot tub. Clay pots are strewn about with calculated nonchalance.

ELEMENTS

PART II

E L E M E N T S
SINKS

The architectural firm of Perkins & Will celebrates the clean lines of a pedestal washbasin by setting it into its own tiled niche. Recessed mirror panel reflects enclosed shower stall along opposite wall. Washbasin, Hastings Tile & Il Bagno Collection; tile, American Olean.

Sinks today are available in a variety of sizes, shapes, colors, materials, and styles. The most commonly available styles are wall-hung, deck-mounted, integral-bowl, and pedestal. Sink backs are available either without holes for fittings or with precut holes to accept four-inch, six-inch, or eight-inch faucet assembles. Standard heights from the floor to the sink rim are thirty-one to thirty-six inches. The most commonly encountered sink materials are vitreous china, synthetic marble, fiberglass-reinforced plastic, acrylic, enameled cast-iron, and enameled steel. Other materials include marble, brass, stainless steel, nickel, and copper.

Wall-hung sinks are the least costly and most compact. They are generally fastened to the wall by means of angle brackets and are best suited to smallish powder rooms and bathrooms.

A self-rimming sink has a molded overlap that is supported by the edge of the countertop cutout. Set inside an undersized mounting hole, the sink rim sits on the countertop, supporting the sink on all sides. This is one of the most popular styles available and is offered in the widest range of shapes to suit any number of styles.

Deck-mounted sinks are available in either flush or unrimmed models. The flush-mounted version features a metal frame that holds the sink to the countertop. The deck-mounted unrimmed style is recessed beneath the countertop and held in place by metal clips. The mounting hole is cut to the size of the bowl, yielding a clean, uncluttered look.

The integral-bowl style is a one-piece molded sink and countertop that sits on top of a vanity or cabinet. The integral bowl and countertop has no joints, which facilitates both installation and cleaning. The units are available in a wide variety of shapes and predrilled holes along the back edge of the sink accept a choice of fittings.

Pedestal sinks in vitreous china feature a selection of sink bowls supported by an upright stem that hides the pipes.

Without the convenience of a vanity cabinet, additional storage considerations must be made. Vanities generally hold the sink, hide the plumbing, and provide storage and counter space; they can be either floor-mounted or cantilevered (wall-hung). Vanities also can be the functional mainstay of the room, offering everything from towel storage to built-in laundry bins.

Pierre Cardin Designs, from Ideal Standard.

"Roma" pedestal lavatory in Sterling Silver color, from American Standard.

"Modern Shape" washbasin and faucet by Abbaka.

This wall-mounted lavatory features a matte-black enamel, ribbed-steel frame, and circular basin insert. The specially designed extra-large, deep basin has a sloped front and vertical back and is available in thirty-two porcelain enamel colors. Design by Heinrich Feldhege. Kroin.

Pedestal washbasin, from American Standard's Warren Platner Collection. ➡

Designed by Heinrich Feldhege, this self-rimming, deep hemispheric basin provides washing convenience without splashing. Fabricated in seamless formed steel, it is available in thirty-two porcelain enamel colors. ◄ Kroin.

Ellisse Whisper Colors™ pedestal washbasin with in-glaze decoration, from American Standard. ►

"Cactus Cutter" suite from Kohler's Artist Limited Editions program.

"Monza" rosewood vanity with Argo Lavatory Set, from Paul Associates.

E L E M E N T S
FITTINGS

"Hydra Deck" tub filler from Paul Associates.

Fittings are sold separately from bath fixtures and are the most frequently used items in a bathroom. The best fittings are cast brass and are available in a variety of plated finishes, including chrome, pewter, enamel, and gold. Some of the newest versions are made completely of plastic and are either brightly colored or chromium-plated. Tap heads are usually made from the same material as the spout, although they also can feature contrasting materials such as acrylic, or even semiprecious stones. Tap shapes range from the streamlined and ultramodern to the traditional, including careful copies of Victorian and Edwardian patterns. There is also a selection of more extravagant fantasy tap sets with swan, dolphin, or even figurine motifs.

Fittings for sinks are available with single, center-set or spread-fit controls. A single-control fitting has a combined faucet and lever or knob that controls water flow and temperature. A center-set control has separate hot-and-cold water controls and a faucet all mounted on a single base. A spread-fit control has separate hot-and-cold water controls and a faucet, each independently mounted and is the least water-efficient. Pop-up stoppers are usually sold separately and are controlled by a lift mechanism in or at the base of the spout.

"Chantal" baked-enamel faucet from Kolson, Inc.

The Fast Fill Double Control Valve was designed by Arne Jacobsen in 1967. The specialized aerated spout supplies nine gallons of water a minute for use with oversize tubs. The double-control valves can be mounted adjacent to or isolated from the supply spout. Available in ten epoxy colors, polished brass, or chrome. Kroin.

This handicap lavatory faucet set features a short fixed spout and specially designed handles that require minimal movement to operate. Hot and cold water supplies are indicated by handle colors. Available in ten epoxy colors, polished brass, or chrome. Kroin.

Whisper Colors™ spread-set faucet from American Standard.

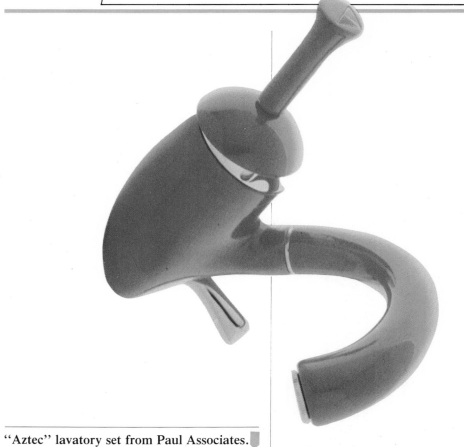

◀ "Orchidea" series washbasin set in red enamel from Watercolors, Inc.

"Aztec" lavatory set from Paul Associates. ▼

The "Roma" lavatory faucet is a spread-set water control with a choice of onyx (green, brown, or ivory) or clear acrylic handles. The eight-inch spout features water-saving aerators and a pop-up drain knob. American Standard. ▼

IV Georges brass lavatory faucet from Kohler.

"Junko" series washbasin set in white enamel from Watercolors, Inc.

The "Principe" line of basin- and deck-mounted fittings features sculpted tap handles and gracefully curved spouts. Fabricated in solid brass, they are available in ten decorative platings and one white-enamel finish. Clockwise, from upper left, deck-mounted tub set with hand spray in Polished Brass; spread-fit basin set with pop-up drain ring; center-set basin fitting with pop-up drain in Ebony finish; spread-fit basin set with pop-up drain in Satin Gold finish; and spread-set bidet fitting with rosette spray and pop-up drain in Copper finish. Hastings Tile & Il Bagno Collection.

WATER CLOSETS & BIDETS

Timothy Hursley

With a reverence usually reserved for more established design icons, this Andy Warhol-designed bathroom contemplates the solitary white-china throne. W.c. unit, American Standard.

Almost exclusively made of vitreous china, water closets vary in style, size, shape, installation, and flushing action. The flushing actions result from bowl design and vary in efficiency.

Wash-down water closets, which are no longer accepted by many code authorities, are the least expensive, least efficient, and most noisy variety. Here the action is characterized by water flushed around the rim of the bowl, allowing the downward force of the water to clear the bowl. A reverse-trap water closet is less noisy than the washdown version, due to its smaller water area, water seal, and trapway; predictably, it is also more costly.

A siphon-jet water closet is still quieter and features a larger water surface. This type of flushing action uses suction to clear the bowl. With an eye for durability, the larger trapways of these bowls also are less likely to clog.

The most efficient and quietest style, however, is the siphon-action water closet. Available as a single-piece unit, this type of bowl offers the largest water surface.

In response to growing environmental concerns, water-saver models are designed with smaller tanks and shallow traps. A single flush of a conventional unit uses seven gallons of water; the water-saver models consume about one-third less water without a loss of efficiency. They are currently available in floor-mounted, wall-hung, one-piece, and two-piece styles. As a rule, their flushing action is either reverse-trap or siphon-vortex.

One-piece water closets are characterized by their low profiles. Designed for floor- and wall-mounting applications, these units generally measure from nineteen to twenty-six inches high with either round or elongated bowls. One-piece models are available with either reverse-trap, siphon-jet, or siphon-action flushing.

Less costly two-piece water closets are also made for either floor-mounting or wall-mounting applications. The wall-hung models, however, are available only in siphon-jet and siphon-action models and require specialized wall-framing to support the weight of the unit (the same is true of the one-piece wall-mounted unit).

Another version of the two-piece water closet is the back outlet, which features an above-floor drain. It is most frequently used on concrete floors, where it would be difficult and costly to install other models.

Although not as frequently seen in the United States as in European countries, the bidet is gaining popularity in American bathrooms. Like water closets, bidets are usually made of vitreous china. They are available in either wall- or deck-mounted versions and feature their own water controls. A variety of spray actions is also offered, with either a spout or vertical spray located in the center of the bowl. Most models also have a pop-up stopper, which allows the unit to double as a footbath.

Arkipelag bath suite from Gustavsberg U.S.A. Inc.

"Ariete" bidet from Hastings Tile & Il Bagno Collection. ➡

W.c. from American Standard's Warren Platner Collection.

"Roma" one-piece from American Standard.

W.c. and bidet from Kohler.

The "Ariete" two-siphon jet water closet features a rounded bowl and tank design. The molded vitreous china unit utilizes an all American-made flushing mechanism, consumes less than three-and-a-half gallons per flush—half the normal amount—and maintains a high-water level. Available in ten colors. Hastings Tile & Il Bagno Collection.

ELEMENTS

TUBS & WHIRLPOOLS

Jaime Ardiles-Arce

New and more comfortable tub sizes and shapes have made the standard bathtub a thing of the past. Most manufacturers make tubs—which are available in an endless array of colors—for three types of installation: recessed, platform, and corner.

Rectangular tubs are available in either recessed or corner models. Recessed tubs fit between two side walls and a back wall and feature one finished side. Corner styles have a finished side and one finished end and fit between a side and back wall. While the corner tub may be right- or left-handed, the interiors of both versions may be oval or rectangular.

Both square- and receptor-style tubs are available for recessed or corner installation. Square tubs are most commonly four-feet-square but can be custom-designed larger.

Sunken tubs can be installed one of two ways: either set in a raised platform or sunk

Designers Robert Bray and Michael Schaible used a tiled platform to elevate this oversized hospital tub to windowsill height. Fittings are mounted along the face of an integral sculpture pedestal. Tub and fittings are from Kohler.

into the floor. This type of tub is available in a variety of contoured shapes and styles and features a molded overlap that is supported by the platform cutout. Generally specified in more spacious applications, platform or sunken tubs are most commonly available in fiberglass, enameled cast iron, or acrylic.

Soaking tubs are the result of Japan's transoceanic design influence. They generally feature deep interiors. Ideal for use in small spaces, they are available in recessed, platform, and corner models with either round or rectangular interiors. Gen-

erally fabricated in acrylic or fiberglass, some models even feature a built-in seating ledge.

Tubs can also be purchased as whirlpool baths, which give the body a massage by means of hydro-air jets delivered from nozzles set at various points around the inside of the bath. Water is drawn from the bath, mixed with air, and delivered back again as a fast-moving stream of aerated water. The number of nozzles will vary according to the model. Whirlpool baths tend to be wider and deeper than ordinary bathtubs to allow the complete immersion necessary to get the full benefit from the massage. Deluxe models will feature timers to automatically control the length and intensity of the massage.

A last word about whirlpools: Like sunken tubs they require extra framing for proper installation and also may require an extra-capacity heater because of their size.

Whirlpool tub from American Standard's Warren Platner Collection.

The Prima II™ by Jacuzzi Whirlpool Bath.

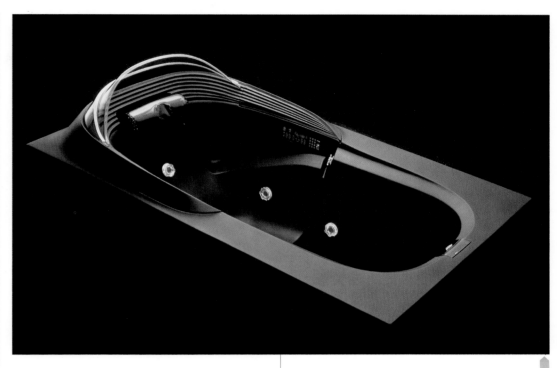

The "Constellation" is a spacious seventy-five-inch drop-in oval whirlpool bath that can easily accommodate two persons. Vacuum-formed from smooth, heavy-gauge acrylic, the base material has a low heat-resistance, which helps retain bathwater temperature. The "Constellation" is available in six colors with matching multidirectional jets. Hastings Tile & Il Bagno Collection.

Electronically controlled "Bath Womb" whirlpool from WaterJet.

"Daphne" is a European-designed bath with anatomical lumbar contours and extra depth for soaking comfort. It is available in five-foot, five-foot-seven, and six-foot lengths, with an optional eight-jet whirlpool system. The self-rimming tub is made of fifteen-gauge steel with a bright enamel finish and features armrests, an antislip bottom, and soundproofing. Hastings Tile & Il Bagno Collection.

TILE

Tile is distinguished as a recognized art form that also doubles as a durable wall and floor treatment. Ceramic tile is one of the most practical and popular surface materials for bathroom walls and floors. Made of hard-fired slabs of clay, ceramic tile is long-lasting, fireproof, impervious to moisture, and easy to maintain. It is available either glazed or unglazed, in an endless array of colors and designs and in a variety of shapes. In glazed tiles, color is applied to the surface before the tiles are fired at high heat. They are available in a variety of finishes, including high-gloss, satin, or pebbly-textured. In unglazed tile, color runs throughout the body, since pigments are mixed with the clay prior to forming and baking. Ceramic mosaic tile is the smallest type of tile available. Its small size makes it very versatile, and it therefore can be installed along curved or tight spaces.

Floor tiles are generally thicker than wall tiles, making them more durable underfoot. They are commonly classified as quarries and pavers and can be glazed or unglazed. Unglazed tile has an advantage in floor use because it is less slippery than

Designer Noel Jeffrey used beveled-edge partitions to architecturally clarify this spalike bathroom. Mixed-tile formats include high-gloss rectangular pavers in cobalt blue from Hastings on the back wall and matte-finished squares from American Olean for the rest of the space.

glazed tile and shows less wear, as its color runs all the way through. If glazed tiles are preferred for the floor, it is best to specify one with a textured or matte surface for better traction and longer wear.

Quarry tiles are usually unglazed in clay colors (beige, black, or red), but can also be had with colorful glazed surfaces. Surface sizes range from six-inch squares to sixteen-inch squares. Its rough surface makes quarry tile a good choice for both indoor and outdoor baths. They must, however, be sealed to avoid staining.

Like most quarry tiles, pavers are unglazed. These rugged tiles come in many colors and are available in three standard sizes: four-inch squares, six-inch squares, and four-by-eight-inch rectangles.

Wall tiles are most commonly glazed and are lighter and thinner than floor tiles. They also are used on ceilings and countertops. Standard sizes for wall tiles range from three-inch squares to four-and-one-half-by-eight-and-one-half-inch rectangles. Many of the wall tiles come with matching trim pieces for edges, coves, and corners. Wall tiles are also available in pregrouted panels for easy installation.

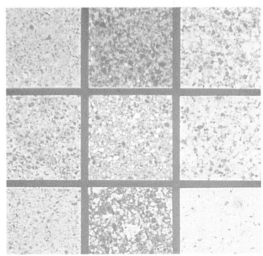

Colored, unsanded grouts from W.R. Bonsal Company.

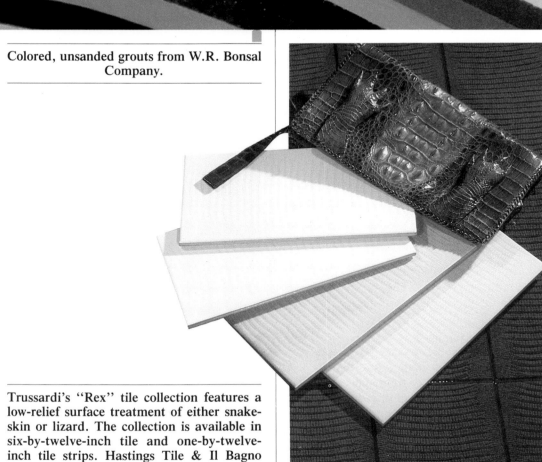

Armstone cast-stone floor tiles and wall panels are over ninety percent marble in combination with a proprietary polymer system. The tiles are manufactured in twelve-inch squares in a three-eighths-inch gauge for flooring applications, and in four-foot-square panels in a three-fourths-inch gauge for wall applications. Armstone tile and panels are available in eighteen natural marble colorways, with a polished or matte finish.

Trussardi's "Rex" tile collection features a low-relief surface treatment of either snakeskin or lizard. The collection is available in six-by-twelve-inch tile and one-by-twelve-inch tile strips. Hastings Tile & Il Bagno Collection.

"Serie Colours" Italian ceramic tile by Rex Ceramiche Spa.

Italian ceramic tile clockwise from top, by Sant' Agostino (red pinstripe), Bardelli (blue/white abstract and solid blue), Nemo Tile Collection (outline stripes), Marazzi (blue grid and yellow zig-zag), Bardelli (red pinstripes), Grazia (red, glossy molding), Bardelli (wavy, multicolored lines), Faver (turquoise square), Faetano (red angled band), Bardelli (diagonal grid), Faver (glossy red square), Bardelli (narrow, yellow stripes), and Piemme (small, multicolor squares on white).

"Traccia" is a glazed ceramic tile that features a ribbed, bas-relief surface design. The vibrational reaction of light and shade on the tile surface highlights the grooves and enhances its dimension. "Traccia" is available in eight colors and four formats: "Traccia 1," twenty-by-twenty inches, in bas-relief with diagonal grooves; "Traccia 2," thirteen-by-twenty-six inches, in heavy-relief with parallel grooves at the bottom edge of the tile; "Traccia 3" and "Traccia 4," thirteen-by-twenty-six inches, in bas-relief with parallel grooves at the top edge of the tile. These can be used in any combination. Hastings Tile & Il Bagno Collection.

Italian ceramic tile clockwise from top, by Faetano, Musa, Campeginese, and Piemme.

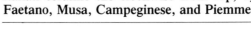

"Porcelain Naturals" from Hastings Tile & Il Bagno Collection.

Whisper Colors™ tile from American Olean.

ELEMENTS
ACCESSORIES

In addition to the variety of fittings, fixtures, wall and floor coverings, there is also an extensive range of accessories available to enhance the bath. The most common items that come to mind include soapdishes, mug and glass holders, towel rails, clothing hooks, waste bins, locks and handles, magazine racks, and, if space permits, even seating.

Of course, changing accessories is the easiest and least expensive way of updating your bath. Newly popularized coordinated lines usually include towel rails, bathroom tissue holders, facial tissue dispensers, soapdishes, toothbrush holders, and sometimes even medicine cabinets and magazine racks. Matching nonstorage items such as electrical outlet covers and drawer pulls are sometimes offered, too. Available in a variety of styles and price ranges, coordinated accessories are available in such materials as plastic, chrome, brass, enamel, and wood. Other coordinated lines include such soft goods as shower curtains, towels, and window treatments.

The soapdish is probably the one single accessory common to most bathrooms. These, of course, are available in styles,

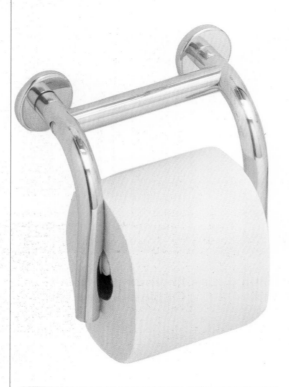

Coordinated tubular brass accessories from Chicago Faucet.

materials, and colors to suit every bathroom decor. There are standard countertop dishes, pedestal models, and wall-mounted units. Materials include ceramic, acrylic, glass, stone, rubber, and even wood. Most dish designs include holes or slats to facilitate drainage and save soap. Separate ribbed or spiked insets are available especially for this purpose.

Towel rails are common to most bathrooms as well. Period styles are usually fabricated in finely worked brass, steel, wood, porcelain, and sometimes even crystal. Contemporary models are considerably simpler, with the most popular choice being the tubular pipe railing with bent corners. Heated towel racks, long popular in Europe, are finally gaining widespread recognition in this country.

Grab bars have become a more popular safety accessory and as such are a lot more evident in shower stalls and beside bathtubs.

Storage accessories can help organize underutilized cabinet space. Lazy Susans, bleacher steps, caddies, racks, stacking sets, and corrals are all available at retail or can be specially designed by a professional.

"Prestige Series" towel bar in gray enamel from Watercolors, Inc.

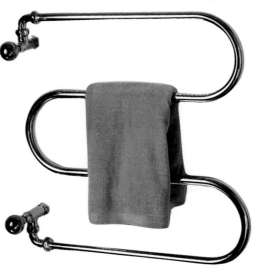

Heated towel bar from Paul Associates.

This single and double toilet roll-holder and kitchen roll-holder were all designed as part of an all-brass modular plumbing system of coordinated mixing valves, outlets, and plates. Designed by Arne Jacobsen, these accessories are available in ten epoxy colors, polished brass, or chrome. Kroin.

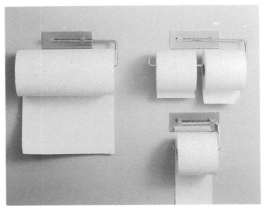

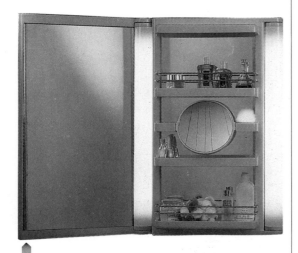

The "Triforo" medicine cabinet from Tulli Zuccari features vertical fluorescent light strips and pivoting side mirrors with open shelf backs. Hastings Tile & Il Bagno Collection.

The toothpaste-tube holder, cup, and toothbrush holder are designed to permit a wide variety of mounting alternatives. Part of an all-brass modular plumbing system, these accessories were designed by Arne Jacobsen. Available in ten epoxy colors, polished brass, or chrome. Kroin.

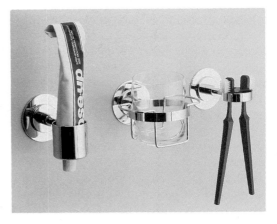

Shower stalls come in a variety of shapes, including square, rectangular, circular, and corner. Both shower and tub/shower kits can be purchased with or without overlapping wall panels, adhesive, and caulking. Kits can also be purchased to use with existing shower bases and tubs. Units are available in fiberglass-reinforced plastic, acrylic, plastic laminate, and synthetic marble.

Shower surrounds in fiberglass-reinforced plastic generally incorporate the shower base and are available in a wide range of colors. Wall panels may include molded soapdishes, ledges, and grab bars. Some models also are available with a ceiling. For minimum comfort, the shower should measure at least three-feet square and at least eighty-four inches high. Corner and circular showers feature clear or tinted acrylic doors that also function as walls.

Shower bases can be purchased separately or in a kit that includes a shower surround. Most bases are made of fiberglass, acrylic, or terrazzo and come in standard sizes in rectangular, square, and corner models with a predrilled drain hole.

Doors for showers come in a variety of styles, including swinging, sliding, folding, and pivoting. Doors and enclosures are commonly made of tempered safety glass with aluminum frames.

Water-saver shower heads are new to the market, while single-control fittings with pressure-balancing and thermostatic valves can also be purchased. Hand-held shower attachments have become increasingly popular in emulation of the European fittings.

In addition to taking a steam in a shower, homeowners today have the option of steaming in a sauna. Once the exclusive domain of the commercial health club, saunas are now making their way into the

ELEMENTS
SHOWERS & SAUNAS

Designers Scott Bromley and Robin Jacobsen created this windowed shower in a midtown New York City loft. A low-tiled ledge holds bath essentials and doubles as a convenient bench. Fittings, Kroin; tile, Orion Nova.

home. Although the sauna can be enjoyed for its own curative benefits, its full physical benefit is realized when it is incorporated into a complete fitness program.

Home installation of a sauna requires adequate space, power, water supply, and drainage, as well as all the mechanical fittings necessary for operation. A seven-foot ceiling is the minimum recommended height for adequate air convection. Various seating levels inside the sauna will coincide with heat levels available to the user. Since heat rises, a lower level seat will be cooler than a higher seat. Heat variation, therefore, will depend on the size of the sauna.

Saunas are nearly all made of wood. The wood must be seasoned and as soft as possible, which in turn makes it cooler for sitting. Considering the stresses of temperature and humidity, it is easy to see why poor quality wood will warp. There are two basic types of construction—log and panel—both of which are adaptable to custom-built specifications.

Log saunas are built from squared poles laid horizontally on top of each other, with the ends extending out from each wall. Panel saunas have a basic wooden skeleton covered with narrow planks running horizontally and vertically. Panel designs have better insulation and heat-retaining properties, while log designs offer better heat distribution due to air circulation through the gaps between the logs.

Electrical or gas heaters lie under a bed of peridotite rocks and heat them. They are then soaked with water to fill the sauna with steam. Successive soakings raise the temperature and humidity to the level required. Floor drainage must be sufficient to collect any water spillage or condensation, and it is essential that interior lighting is waterproof and electrically safe.

The Habitat Masterbath™ total environment from Kohler.

"Raindrop" personal shower with flexible hose from Kohler.

Corner shower cabinet from Teuco features a molded seat, storage niche, and clear acrylic panels. The shower head is equipped with a flexible hose that permits hand-held usage. Available in eight colors. Hastings Tile & Il Bagno Collection. ▶

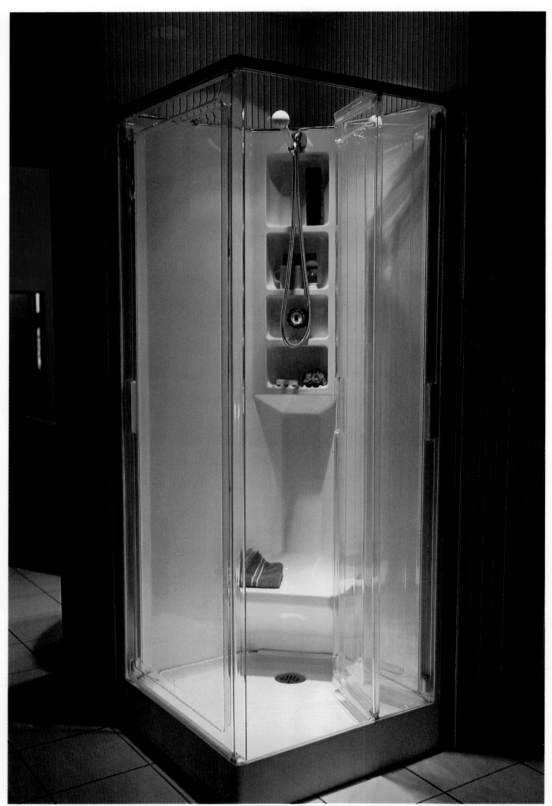

This round bathtub with wall fittings and curved acrylic water shield is from Teuco. The wall panel conveniently organizes towel and shelf storage as well as the hand-held shower and water controls. Available in eight colors. Hastings Tile & Il Bagno Collection.

Once the exclusive domain of the health club, saunas are becoming more common on the home front. The panel sauna, top, created by Dexter Design, features double-tiered benches that allow users to enjoy different temperature levels within the same unit. The wall-mounted heater is safely enclosed in a wooden frame while the oversize porthole in the door relieves the feeling of enclosure.

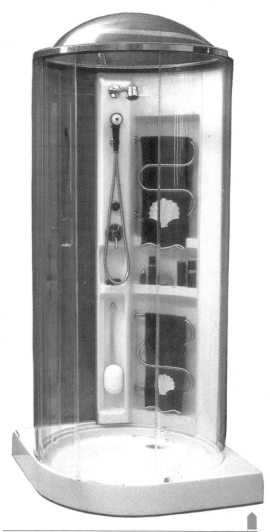

With an angled base, this round shower from Teuco is for corner applications. Available in eight colors, this model features built-in tubular towel bars, a storage shelf, and hand-held shower attachment with removable mount. Hastings Tile & Il Bagno Collection.

RESOURCES

What are the design steps?

Here are some of the preliminary steps the home designer must take before actually beginning work on the bathroom.

☐ Consider building codes and permits. Some building codes require minimum clearance distances between bath fixtures such as toilets, sinks, and showers. A building permit may also be needed for some extensive jobs that require major construction changes or involve plumbing and electrical work. Check with the local building department before proceeding with any work.

☐ Make a rough drawing of the room, allowing enough space on the drawing so that dimensions can easily be inserted. Use two basic plans: the floor plan and the wall plan. Use the measurements of feet and inches.

☐ Draw to scale, using the conversion ¼ inch = 1 foot. Measure the actual room with a steel rule, recording information on graph paper with an architect's scale.

☐ Detail the project plans by adding positions and dimensions of elements and fixtures such as counters, windows, and shelving.

☐ Use the information in this book to become familiar with available products and project designs. Then carefully survey the bathroom to determine which ideas are most applicable to the space.

☐ Make notes of possible electrical wiring, plumbing, heating systems, ventilation, and other constructional changes. Consider if such changes will involve walls, floors, and ceilings and how such work can be avoided wherever possible.

☐ Designate a place to store information, samples, swatches, product literature, layout, and plans.

Is it safe?

The bathroom can be the most dangerous room of the house if certain precautions

PROJECT CHECKLIST

are not taken at appropriate stages of planning.

☐ Position electrical outlets out of arm's reach of tub or shower. Equip outlets with circuit breakers.

☐ Choose water fixtures that are reliable and adjust to desired temperature quickly and accurately. Lower the setting of the water heater or install a mixing valve that will prevent unexpected water-temperature changes. Be aware that burning hot water can cause a severe burn within 3 seconds.

☐ Choose a nonslip surface for floors and also for the shower and tub. For additional safety, a rail-grip accessory can be installed in the shower or tub.

☐ Include safety latches on cabinetry and storage areas so that children cannot get their hands on chemicals and drugs.

Is it energy-efficient and functional?

Besides being beautiful, a bathroom should be energy-efficient and functional. Consider the following points before finalizing any plans.

☐ Sometimes preexisting fittings already serve the purpose. However, keep in mind that the initial investment for new, water-efficient fittings will most likely pay for itself. Many of the fittings showcased in this book are equipped with flow-control devices; some even aerate water to give it more force, but save water at the same time.

☐ Look for water-saving toilets that use 3–3½ gallons per flush, compared to the standard amount of 5–7 gallons.

☐ Be sure that all of the elements you choose for your bathroom are easy to maintain. Recommended materials are glass, marble, glazed ceramic tile, vitreous china, plastic laminate, porcelain enameled steel, and cast iron.

☐ Be sure that wood used for saunas is high quality, and, preferably, polyurethaned. Wood tends to discolor and warp if it is not able to withstand heat and moisture.

When is outside help needed?

There are some jobs that are just too big for a house or apartment dweller to design or complete alone.

☐ To consult an architect or designer, use this book's reference section as a source. The AIA (American Institute of Architects) or the AIBD (American Institute of Building Design) will most likely be able to help locate a professional.

☐ Often, a designer or architect will oversee the work of a contractor or subcontractor.

☐ Some home designers prefer to go directly to a contractor. Get bids from several sources, and then work out an agreement that includes total costs and a payment schedule.

What is future-minded planning?

Whirlpools are fast becoming the standard luxury item of the future. For those who like to plan ahead, keep these ideas in mind.

☐ Remember that all whirlpools are bathtubs attached to an electrical pump. The pump injects air and water into the tub through jets located in the sides. Each stream's force is determined by the motor and number of jets. For a single-sized tub, the force should be at least ½ horsepower. A suction device then circulates aerated water that travels more quickly than ordinary water.

☐Whirlpools come in many shapes and sizes, the least expensive ranging from $1,000 to $1,500 for a single-sized model. Double-sized models range from $2,000 to $3,000, while models made to hold 3 or more people start at $3,500, and can reach prices of $10,000. Of course, the price can be escalated by features such as brass piping, marble or onyx finish, gold-plated fixtures, and other sybaritic amenities.

☐The models that feature fiberglass coated with polyester gel scratch easily.

☐Designers recommend choosing light colors for whirlpools, since darker colors tend to show water stains.

☐Models with cast-iron shells impart a pleasing, cool touch.

☐Don't count on the base price to be the total price. Ask about the installation costs too.

☐Some tubs are retrofitted and work well in small-space bathrooms; they fit into standard spaces to replace old tubs. But be sure to select a tub that is at least 18" deep if the length of the shell is less than 5 feet, to ensure that the water fully covers the submerged body.

☐City dwellers will probably need to get permission from the landlord or cooperative board of the building before installing a tub.

☐Make sure the floor can withstand the weight of the tub, particularly with people in it. Also measure the hallways and doorways of the home to make sure the tub will fit into the apartment or house.

☐Water pressure must be strong enough to fill the tub quickly before cooling occurs. Most bathroom plumbing systems have ¾-inch diameter pipes, narrowing into ½-inch pipes for the tub. For a whirlpool, the pipes that lead to the tub to be at least ¾ inches in diameter, and the water-filler spout must be larger than the usual size, or several small spouts may be employed to get the job done adequately.

Carpet

ROSESCORE CARPET CO.
979 Third Ave.
New York, N.Y. 10022
(212) 752–8013

STARK CARPET CORP.
979 Third Ave.
New York, N.Y. 10022
(212) 752–9000

Fabrics, Towels, & Wallcoverings

BRUNSCHWIG & FILS, INC.
979 Third Ave.
New York, N.Y. 10022
(212) 838–7878

ROSE CUMMING, INC.
232 E. 59th St.
New York, N.Y. 10022
(212) 758–0844

FONTHILL WALLPAPER LTD.
30 W. 26th St.
New York, N.Y. 10010
(212) 924–3000

YVES GONNET, INC.
D & D Bldg.
979 Third Ave.
New York, N.Y. 10022
(212) 758–8220

LERON, INC.
745 Fifth Ave.
New York, N.Y. 10151
(212) 753–6700

MANUFACTURERS & RETAILERS

HALSTON ENTERPRISES INC.
645 Fifth Ave.
New York, N.Y. 10114
(212) 980–4800

D. PORTHAULT, INC.
57 E. 57th St.
New York, N.Y. 10022
(212) 688–1660

QUADRILLE WALLPAPERS & FABRICS, INC.
979 Third Ave.
New York, N.Y. 10022
(212) 753–2995

ROSECORE HANDPRINTS
979 Third Ave.
New York, N.Y. 10022
(212) 752–8013

SCALAMANDRE WALLPAPER
950 Third Ave.
New York, N.Y. 10022
(718) 361–8500

Fittings

ARTISTIC BRASS
4100 Ardmore Ave.
South Gate, Calif. 90280
(213) 564–1100

CHICAGO FAUCET CO.
2100 S. Nuclear Dr.
Des Plaines, Ill. 60018
(312) 694–4400

DELTA FAUCET CO.
55 E. 111th St.
Box 40980
Indianapolis, Ind. 46280
(317) 848–1812

KARTELL U.S.A.
225 Fifth Ave.
New York, N.Y. 10010
(212) 889–9111

KRAFT HARDWARE, INC.
306 E. 61st St.
New York, N.Y. 10021
(212) 838–2214

SPEAKMAN
Box 191
Wilmington, Del. 19899
(302) 764–7100

U.S. BRASS
901 Tenth St.
Plano, Tex. 75074
(214) 423–3576

Fixtures

ABBAKA
435—23rd St.
San Francisco, Calif. 94107
(212) 750–9189

AMEREC CORP.
Box 3825
Bellevue, Wa. 98009
(206) 643–2000

AMERICAN-STANDARD INC.
40 W. 40th St.
New York, N.Y. 10036
(212) 840–5100

AQUA BATHS, INC.
351 W. Broadway
New York, N.Y. 10011
(212) 924–8282

CRANE PLUMBING & FIAT PRODUCTS
2020 Dempster Pl.
Suite 1235
Evanston, Ill. 60202
(312) 864–7600

ELKAY MFG. CO.
2335 Boston Post Rd.
Larchmont, N.Y. 10538
(914) 834–6800

P.E. GUERIN
23 Jane St.
New York, N.Y. 10014
(212) 243–5270

HASTINGS II BAGNO COLLECTION
201 E. 57th St.
New York, N.Y. 10022
(212) 755–2710

JACUZZI WHIRLPOOL BATH
P.O. Drawer J
Dept. HG
Walnut Creek, Calif. 94596
Calif.:
(800) 227–0991
elsewhere:
(800) 227–0710

JACUZZI WHIRLPOOL BATH
LUMIERE COLLECTION
P.O. Drawer J
Walnut Creek, Calif. 95956
Calif., Ala., Hawaii:
(415) 938–7070
elsewhere:
(800) 227–0710
(baths, bidets, lavatories)

KOHLER CO.
Kohler, Wis. 53044
(414) 457–4441

KOLSON INC.
653 Middle Neck Rd.
Great Neck, N.Y. 11023
(516) 829–4150

PAUL ASSOCIATES, INC.
155 E. 55 St.
New York, N.Y. 10022
(212) 755–1313

POGGENPOHL U.S.A. CORP.
6 Pearl Ct.
Allendale, N.J. 07401
(201) 934–1511

SMOLKA CO., INC.
182 Madison Ave.
New York, N.Y. 10016
(212) 679–2700

SHERLE WAGNER
INTERNATIONAL, INC.
60 E. 57th St.
New York, N.Y. 10022
(212) 758–3300

WATER JET CORP.
8431 Canoga Ave.
Canoga Park, Calif. 91304
(818) 998–3884

WILSONART
600 General Bruce Dr.
Temple, Tex. 76501
(817) 777–2711

Furniture, Objects, & Accessories

MARVIN ALEXANDER
315 E. 62nd St.
New York, N.Y. 10021
(212) 838–2320

ATELIER INTERNATIONAL LTD.
595 Madison Ave.
New York, N.Y. 10022
(212) 644–0400

BIELECKY BROS. INC.
306 E. 61st St.
New York, N.Y. 10021
(212) 753–2355

DAKOTA JACKSON
306 E. 61st St.
New York, N.Y. 10021
(212) 838–9444

KARTELL U.S.A.
225 Fifth Ave.
New York, N.Y. 10010
(212) 889–9111

OBJETS PLUS, INC.
315 E. 62nd St.
New York, N.Y. 10021
(212) 832–3386

KARL SPRINGER LTD.
306 E. 61st St.
New York, N.Y. 10021
(212) 752–1695

SHERLE WAGNER
INTERNATIONAL, INC.
60 E. 57th St.
New York, N.Y. 10022
(212) 758–3300

WATERCOLORS, INC.
Garrison, N.Y. 10524
(914) 424–3327

Lighting Fixtures & Design

ARCHITEL SYSTEMS
251 Park Ave. South
New York, N.Y. 10010
(212) 475–0900

HARRY GITLIN
121 W. 19th St.
New York, N.Y. 10011
(212) 243–1080

HANSEN LAMPS
121 E. 24th St.
New York, N.Y. 10010
(212) 674–2130

KA-LOR CUBICLE
(mailing address only)
Box 804
Fair Lawn, N.J. 07410

LIGHTING DESIGN INC.
141 W. 24th St.
New York, N.Y. 10011
(212) 924–4050

LIGHTOLIER INC.
1071 Ave. of the Americas
New York, N.Y. 10018
(212) 719–1616

Surface Treatments

DU PONT CO.
1007 Market St.
Wilmington, Del. 19898
(800) 441–7515

FORMICA CORP.
1 Cyanamid Plaza
Wayne, N.J. 07470
(800) 524–0159

Tile

AMERICAN OLEAN TILE CO.
1000 Cannon Ave.
Lansdale, Pa. 19446
(215) 855–1111

ARMSTRONG INDUSTRY CORP.
1637A Hillside Ave.
New Hyde Park, N.Y. 11040
(718) 347–0880

W.R. BONSAL CO.
8201 Arrowridge Blvd.
Box 241148
Charlotte, N.C. 28224
(704) 525–1621

COUNTRY FLOORS INC.
300 E. 61st St.
New York, N.Y. 10021
(212) 758–7414

DESIGN TECHNICS CERAMICS
INC.
160 E. 56th St.
New York, N.Y. 10022
(212) 355–3183

HASTINGS TILE & II BAGNO
COLLECTION
201 E. 57th St.
New York, N.Y. 10022
(212) 755–2710

ITALIAN CERAMIC TILE CTR.
499 Park Ave.
New York, N.Y. 10021
(212) 980–8866

MARBLE TECHNICS
150 E. 58th St.
New York, N.Y. 10155
(212) 750–9189

SMOLKA CO., INC.
182 Madison Ave.
New York, N.Y. 10016
(212) 679–2700

SUMMITVILLE TILES INC.
Summitville, Ohio 43962
(216) 223–1511

PROFESSIONAL ORGANIZATIONS

AMERICAN INSTITUTE OF
ARCHITECTS
1735 New York Ave. Northwest
Washington, D.C. 20006
(202) 626–7300

AMERICAN INSTITUTE OF
BUILDING DESIGN
1412—19th St.
Sacramento, Calif. 95814
(916) 447–2422

AMERICAN SOCIETY OF
INTERIOR DESIGNERS
4620 Wisconsin Ave. Northwest
Washington, D.C. 20016
(202) 686–5467

DESIGNERS

BELCIC & JACOBS
157 W. 57th St.
New York, N.Y. 10019
(212) 541–5770

ERIC BERNARD
177 E. 94th St.
New York, N.Y. 10128
(212) 876–9295

LAURA BOHN
LEMBO-BOHN ASSOCIATES
116 W. 29th St.
New York, N.Y. 10010
(212) 947–0547

BRAY-SCHAIBLE DESIGNS INC.
80 W. 40th St.
New York, N.Y. 10018
(212) 354–7525

RONALD BRICKE
333 E. 69th St.
New York, N.Y. 10021
(212) 472–9006

BROMLEY/JACOBSEN
ARCHITECTURE & DESIGN
242 W. 27th St.
New York, N.Y. 10001
(212) 620–4250

RUSSELL CECIL
330 E. 59th St.
New York, N.Y. 10022
(212) 832–8621

ALAN BUCHSBAUM
DESIGN COALITION
12 Greene St.
New York, N.Y. 10013
(212) 966–3010

RUBÉN DE SAAVEDRA, ASID
225 E. 57th St.
New York, N.Y. 10022
(212) 759–2892

DENNING & FOURCADE INC.
125 E. 73rd St.
New York, N.Y. 10021
(212) 759–1969

dePOLO/DUNBAR INC.
330 W. 42nd St.
New York, N.Y. 10036
(212) 947–6645

DEXTER DESIGN INC.
133 E. 58th St.
New York, N.Y. 10022
(212) 752–2426

MARY DIAL
1 Sutton Pl. South
New York, N.Y. 10022
(212) 371–2144

ANGELO DONGHIA
315 E. 62nd St.
New York, N.Y. 10022
(212) 838–9100

ROBERT DREW
130 St. Marks Pl.
New York, N.Y. 10003
(212) 982–3914

BRAD ELIAS
HOCHEISER-ELIAS DESIGN
GROUP, INC.
322 E. 86th St.
New York, N.Y. 10028
(212) 535–7437

ARTHUR ERICKSON
125 N. Robertson Blvd.
Los Angeles, Calif. 90048
(213) 278–1915

FREDERICK FISHER
1422A 2nd St.
Santa Monica, Calif. 90401
(213) 451–1767

STANLEY JAY FRIEDMAN, INC.
200 East 71st St.
New York, NY 10021
(212) 988–3595

GILLIS ASSOCIATES
156 Fifth Ave.
New York, N.Y. 10010
(212) 243–5330

PETER GLUCK
19 Union Sq. West
New York, N.Y. 10003
(212) 255–1876

GWATHMEY-SIEGEL &
ASSOCIATES
475 Tenth Ave.
New York, N.Y. 10018
(212) 947–1240

STEPHEN HOLL
655 Sixth Ave.
New York, N.Y. 10010
(212) 989–0918

INTRATECH GROUP LTD.
30 Waterside Plaza
New York, N.Y. 10010
(212) 889–8992

KEMP & SIMMERS
1160 Park Ave.
New York, N.Y. 10128
(212) 534–6754

CHARLES KREWSON
1113 Madison Ave.
New York, N.Y. 10028
(212) 628–6054

PAUL LEONARD
Rte. 199
Roxbury, Conn. 06783
(203) 354–0107

RICHARD LOWELL NEAS
157 E. 71st St.
New York, N.Y. 10021
(212) 772–4878

MARSHALL-SCHULE
ASSOCIATES
220 E. 73rd St.
New York, N.Y. 10021
(212) 868–1616

WILLIAM E. MILLER
311 E. 23rd St.
New York, N.Y. 10010
(212) 532–1662

JOHN ROBERT MOORE
41 E. 68th St.
New York, N.Y. 10021
(212) 249–9370

MORPHOSIS
2113 Stoner Ave.
Los Angeles, Calif. 90401
(213) 477–2674

J. ALLEN MURPHY
575 Park Ave.
New York, N.Y. 10022
(212) 838–4900
(516) 922–4007

GEORGE NAKASHIMA
R.D. 2, Box 16
New Hope, Pa. 18938
(215) 862–2651

TOM O'TOOLE
145 E. 92nd St.
New York, N.Y. 10028
(212) 348–0639

FRED PALATINUS
239 E. 18th St.
New York, N.Y. 10021
(212) 473–7369

PATINO/WOLF ASSOCIATES INC.
400 E. 52nd St.
New York, N.Y. 10022
(212) 355–6581

FLORENCE PERCHUK &
ASSOCIATES
313 W. 37th St.
New York, N.Y. 10018
(212) 239–8210

JOSEF PRICCI
257 E. 72nd St.
New York, N.Y. 10021
(212) 744–4962

REALE-FROJD ASSOCIATES
134 Greene St.
New York, N.Y. 10012
(212) 431–4484

DENNIS ROLLAND
33 E. 61st St.
New York, N.Y. 10021
(212) 644–0537

VALERIAN S. RYBAR, INC.
601 Madison Ave.
New York, N.Y. 10022
(212) 752–1861

JOHN SALADINO
305 E. 63rd St.
New York, N.Y. 10022
(212) 752–2440

MICHAEL TAYLOR INTERIOR
DESIGN
9—25th Ave. North
San Francisco, Calif. 94121
(415) 668–7668

ADAM TIHANY
57–59 E. 11th St.
New York, N.Y. 10003
(212) 505–2360

KEVIN WALZ
WALZ DESIGN INC.
141 Fifth Ave.
New York, N.Y. 10010
(212) 477–2211

BEVERLY WILLIS
WILLIS & ASSOCIATES INC.
545 Mission St.
San Francisco, Calif. 94105
(415) 777–4660

ZAJAC & CALLAHAN
95 Horatio St.
New York, N.Y. 10014
(212) 741–1291

INDEX

PHOTOGRAPHERS

JAIME ARDILES-ARCE
663 Fifth Ave.
New York, N.Y. 10022
(212) 688–9191

ADAM BARTOS
136 Grand St.
New York, N.Y. 10013
(212) 925–1389

JEFF BLECHMAN
591 Broadway
New York, N.Y. 10012
(212) 966–1455

PETER BOSCH
477 Broome St.
New York, N.Y. 10013
(212) 925–0707

GEORGE CSERNA
80 Second Ave.
New York, N.Y. 10003
(212) 477–3472

RICHARD DAVIES
C/O THE WORLD OF INTERIORS
228-230 Fulham Rd.
London, SW10 9NB
England
(01) 351–5177

DANIEL EIFERT
26 Second Ave.
New York, N.Y. 10003
(212) 473–2562

PHILLIP H. ENNIS
PHOTOGRAPHY
8 Makamah Beach Rd.
Northport, N.Y. 11768
(516) 754–2638

ESTO PHOTOGRAPHICS, INC.
222 Valley Pl.
Mamaroneck, N.Y. 10543
(914) 698–4060

ELLIOT FINE
3 Sheridan Sq.
New York, N.Y. 10014
(212) 675–0465

TIMOTHY HURSLEY
THE ARKANSAS OFFICE
115 E. Captiol
Little Rock, Ark. 72201
(501) 372–0640

JAMES LEVIN PHOTOGRAPHY
141 W. 28th St.
New York, N.Y. 10001
(212) 736–1830

ROBERT LEVIN
718 Broadway
New York, N.Y. 10003
(212) 982–9812

NORMAN MCGRATH
PHOTOGRAPHY
164 W. 79th St.
New York, N.Y. 10024
(212) 799–6422

CHARLES NESBIT
156 Fifth Ave.
New York, N.Y. 10010
(212) 242–8846

PETER PAIGE PHOTOGRAPHY
37 W. Homestead Ave.
Palisades Park, N.J. 07650
(201) 592–7889

MARK ROSS PHOTOGRAPHY,
INC.
345 E. 80th St.
New York, N.Y. 10021
(212) 744–7258

BILL STEELE
MATTIELLO-STEELE ASSOCIATES
20 Beekman Pl.
New York, N.Y. 10022
(212) 751–8282

PETER VITALE
208 E. 60th St.
New York, N.Y. 10022
(212) 319–6997

PAUL WARCHOL
PHOTOGRAPHY
18 E. 16th St.
New York, N.Y. 10003
(212) 929–8770

ELIZABETH WHITING
ASSOCIATES
21 Albert St.
London, NW1
England
(01) 388–2828